There I had got the Cape under me, as much as if I were riding it bare-backed. It was not as on the map, or seen from the stage-coach; but there I found it all out of doors, huge and real, Cape Cod! as it cannot be represented on a map, color it as you will; the thing itself, than which there is nothing more like it, no truer picture or account; which you cannot go farther and see.

—Henry David Thoreau, *Cape Cod*

THE CAPE ITSELF

Text by

Robert Finch

Photographs by

Ralph MacKenzie

W. W. Norton & Company
New York • London

The text appearing on page 84 was originally published in *The Primal Place* by Robert Finch. Copyright © 1983 by Robert Finch. Reprinted by permission of W. W. Norton & Company.

The text appearing on pages 143–44, 183, 186 was originally published in *Common Ground* by Robert Finch. Copyright © 1981 by Robert Finch. Reprinted by permission of David R. Godine, Publisher.

The text appearing on pages 39, 41, 144, 186, 189 was originally published in *Outlands* by Robert Finch. Copyright © 1986 by Robert Finch. Reprinted by permission of David R. Godine, Publisher.

Printed in Hong Kong by South China Printing Co.

The text of this book is composed in Palatino.
Composition by Trufont, Inc.
Book design by Katy Homans.

First Edition

Library of Congress Cataloging–in–Publication Data

Finch, Robert, 1943–
MacKenzie, Ralph, 1942–
    The Cape itself / text by Robert Finch ; photographs by Ralph
MacKenzie.
        p.   cm.
    1. Cape Cod (Mass.)—Description and travel.   2. Cape Cod (Mass.)—
Description and travel—Views.   I. MacKenzie, Ralph.   II. Title.
F72.C3F56   1991
974.4'92—dc20   91-2468

ISBN 0-393-02994-8

W. W. Norton & Company, Inc., 500 Fifth Avenue, New York, N.Y. 10110
W. W. Norton & Company, Ltd., 10 Coptic Street, London WC1A 1PU

1 2 3 4 5 6 7 8 9 0

CONTENTS

FOREWORD

THE HUMAN SCALE

Bound Brook Island, Wellfleet

O F ALL THE THINGS that attract us to a place like Cape Cod—and they are many and often indecipherable—nothing has so enduring a hold on us as its human scale. The vast and impersonal ocean excepted, there is little here that can be termed overpowering. The land is all of human dimensions—even the bold, eroding cliffs of the Outer Beach have a visible fragility about them that inspires compassion as much as awe.

We need no astronaut's photo of the earth to sense our own unity and isolation here. From the top of Shoot Flying Hill in Barnstable, from the Marconi Site in Wellfleet, from the top of Mt. Ararat in Provincetown, from any number of places on this peninsula we can stand, Balboa-like, and view water on both sides of us, discerning the sickle-shape of the Cape. It is easy to see for ourselves the extended and circumscribed nature of this land, the tacit covenant of earth and sea by which we maintain our foothold here.

Although it can be violent and fierce in a gale, or inscrutable and even threatening when shrouded in fog, the familiar countenance of Cape Cod is gentle and moderate, even touchingly vulnerable, like a set of cherished features deteriorating in the rain of time. Although it can appear ancient and desolate in places, it is, like us, of recent origin, still young, still forming, still flexing its shape. The preeminent metaphor for the Cape has always been a human arm, beckoning, protective, or threatening, as we choose to see it.

Even changes in the land's features seem to occur on a time scale compatible with our own, rather than on one of geological remoteness. Major alterations in its outline take place within our own lifetimes. It yields and adjusts to the forces that shape it, providing another metaphor for endurance in the face of irresistible stress and pressure. Its living features change as well. Stunted trees that in many places barely top a man's head are only the latest in a series of shifting forest covers. Fish and bird species come and go in response to local and global alterations. Some of its most magnificent "natural" landscapes—such as the dunes of the Provincelands—are in fact intimately wedded to human activities.

Even more than other parts of New England, with which it shares so much, the Cape's landscape is eminently accessible. Its greatest width is less than twenty miles; most of it averages seven or eight miles, and in some places only a few hundred yards of sand hold its parts together. Its highest point barely tops three hundred feet, and less than one hundred is the general rule. Hills climbable, streams fordable, prospects reachable—the Cape "scene" calls for more than passive visual appreciation. It asks active tactile exploration and recognition, which is both its promise and our problem; for as more and more of us accept its promise, the less each of us will be able to touch it.

For over three and a half centuries we have had an intense and visible relationship with Cape Cod. First we farmed and lumbered it intensely, then we fished it intensely, and in the last century we have bogged it, burned it, and, when hunger drove us, berried it intensely. Today we are busy paving, subdividing, malling, and condominiumizing it with an all too blind intensity. "Own a slice of the Cape," the real estate ad says—and watch it bleed.

Because of its human scale and vulnerability, human violation of the land is somehow more glaring here, more outrageous and unacceptable. Yet for all of its accessibility, all of its manageable, encompassable, conquerable dimensions, its secret still eludes us. In one sense this small region has been studied exhaustively: measured and charted, soil-analyzed, water-surveyed, bird-and-wildflower-censused, and so on. And yet after each new study the mystery called Cape Cod turns flukes up and dives out of sight once more.

We know it is there. It continues to draw millions of us seasonally, and thousands more of us permanently each year, though each year there seems to be less and less reason for coming. Poets and artists have caught it sporadically—on dark, moon-flecked tides, in the pulse of its hidden lives, in an astringent toughness of salt and sand somehow capable of cradling the gentlest beauty—but it is never in the same place the next time we look.

What its embraceable dimensions offer us, in the broadest sense, is a chance for human intercourse with nature, a chance to *make with* rather than to exploit or live apart from, a chance to regain or fashion that sense of fitness and harmony with the land which we may once have had and lost, or should have had and are fast losing our opportunities to create.

Thoreau, visiting the Cape during the 1850s, admired it for being "a wild, rank place, [with] no flattery in it." Since his time we have largely subdued its wildness (or so we think), we have civilized its rankness (by replacing it with our own), and God knows we have imported enough flattery. But still it speaks to us, basic nature, in a strangely human voice. Strip off the veneer of our manmade landscape, even peel back a small corner of it—say a bit of the flats at low tide—and the Original Cape, wild, rank, and savingly candid, is still there.

As the "low-lying headland wooded to the brink of the sea" spoke of a new beginning to the Mayflower passengers three hundred and seventy years ago, so it speaks to us today of a return, a refashioning and untwisting of our values, a promise of human fitness in a natural world. Here, more than most places, we can still find the building materials of the spirit at our feet.

Fly trap on Barnstable Marsh

THE WIND OF CREATION

Dune grass, gull, and storm front

I WENT DOWN TO PAINE'S CREEK this evening about six, just past low tide. At the landing a few older couples sat in their cars soaking up the declining sun and drinking martinis. The gulls stood out on the flats, planted like trees. The new marsh grass and channels of water danced outward together in piled layers of shining green and intense blue. Four yellowlegs dipped and promenaded about a tidal pool; another enclosed pool held an aquarium full of chubs.

I walked out beside the tidal creek, still flowing out and only a few inches deep, while the sun, moving northwest, shattered itself in white-gold light on the moving water, and a stiff wind from the same quarter kept me in a tacking relationship to it. From the sandy bank of the creek a huge slab of ship-planking had recently emerged, nearly twenty feet long and heavily encrusted with ancient, empty barnacles.

I continued out on a thick peninsula of exposed mud flat several hundred feet long that was already being narrowed and shortened by the tide. The probing water-fingers crept in between the sand riffles, edged in mud-foam and strung with dark-red tresses of Irish moss, slightly audible in their creeping with the soft susurrus of moving sand.

I found myself thinking of the wind and the tide, and of their constant motion, a motion that has never ceased, here or anywhere, and of how, literally, the wind of creation continues to blow through the universe here. It seems that man's own spiritual history is reflected in this motion, that, like the physical universe itself, the breath of his spirit is diastolic, repeatedly expanding outward from and recontracting toward its source in nature and natural history.

IT IS THE WIND, more than any other force, which gives this place its sense of outpost, of certain exposure and vulnerability to the elements—like that of the Great Plains, but without the stability of a continent around it. Down here the wind blows as a permanent thing, keeping trees, bushes, and grass bent back, vibrating slightly in the steady tension. Some, like the oaks and cedars, spring back in summer, and stand straight once more. Others, like the pitch pine, abandon the wind side and spread to leeward, growing and creeping to the mold of the wind. Marsh grasses weaken at their bases and give, some toppling over like wooden soldiers, others falling in swirls and cowlicks. The fluorescent lights of service stations weave dangerously on their long curved metal stalks, and hold. Even the Cape itself appears as a spring coiled back on itself by northeast storms and steady surf, ready to lash out at the sea once the endless waves abate.

Quahogs dropped on a rock by sea gulls

STEP OUTSIDE FOR A MOMENT. It is very beautiful. The snow of the past two days has crusted and hardened, and tonight the wind is blowing the loose granules, hard and glinting under the full moon, over the frozen drifts. But in the bare, toneless rattle of crabbed oak leaves on the iron limbs, in the cold blue stare of Sirius down on us from a measureless, impersonal distance, in the soft, persistent sough of the wind from the cedars in the swamp, darker than the night itself, one may get very quickly, for a deep moment, a sense of what it was like to lie exposed to this treeless land, night after night, wrapped only in a blanket and seeking the touch of one another's naked flesh for warmth. A chill invades us, and before we realize it we have rushed back inside, to be flooded by artificial warmth and artificial light and artificial music, driving out the cold and the night-wind back into our disgraced past.

I LIVE IN A LAND that will no longer exist in six thousand years or so. That is a remarkable circumstance, one that cannot really be said of very many places of comparable size in the world, and perhaps of none of comparable identity. And what does that, what should that do to one's sense of living here? Six thousand years, sixty centuries, is as much time, roughly, as the wheel is said to have existed. What has the wheel done thus far? What has the wheel done to this place, and what will it do in another six thousand years?

AH, BUT THIS IS A BEAUTIFUL and a mythic place! Out over the protected glacial bluffs the waters of Pleasant Bay stream in on a flood tide; the bay islands lie low and long in sinuous profile, like dinosaurs in a great swamp; seagulls rise up and drop clams on the guano-spattered rocks below; and the sunlight, as always, beneath the fragrant pitch pines, is wet.

THE CAPE IS ONE OF THE YOUNGEST PIECES of North American geography, barely fifteen thousand years old in its present form; yet it is an old, old land in terms of human exploitation. Its waters have been fished for centuries. Portuguese fishermen are said to have taken up temporary residence on the shores of Province-town Harbor over three hundred years before their "descendants" settled permanently there in the 1800s. Even before the great westward push into New England began in the late 1600s, a backwater movement from the Plymouth toehold to the

Boat traffic

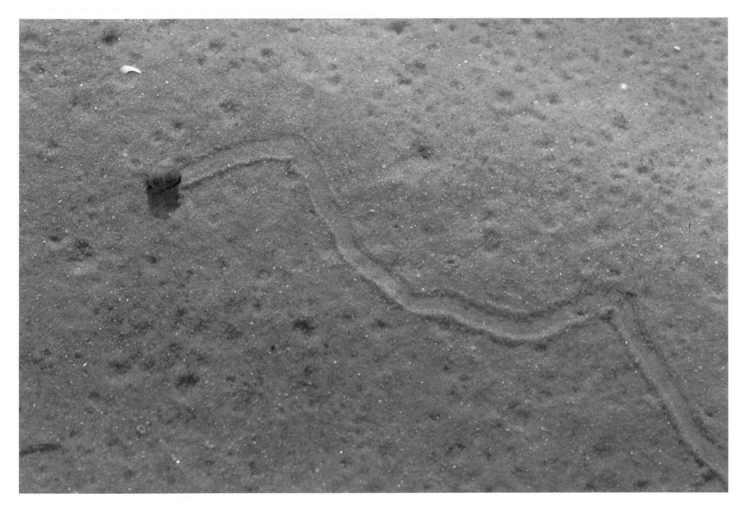

Underwater snail trail

Cape had begun, settling the early towns of Sandwich, Barnstable, and Eastham. The trees have been hacked down, again and again, so that they have a dwarfed, grotesque look now, "sprout hardwood," useless for lumber. The streams, though few, are clear-running, the soil having been blown and eroded away so completely and so long ago that it no longer muddies them.

Yet despite this, and despite the creeping blight of development, the Cape as a whole still wears a pristine, new-minted look, as fresh as its first morning. Its fragility is in part resilience, for it holds its scars and bears its grudges less than most places, or, as in the case of the dunes, transforms our abuses into new shapes. Unlike the stripped and eroded coal lands of Appalachia, say, or the gouged minelands of the West, the Cape heals quickly, because it yields easily. It seems to have an inner speed and elasticity it has borrowed from the sea that surrounds it, and which enables it to rejuvenate itself, to compensate for and keep up with the antiquity and intensity of its use.

THIS IS A PLACE OF SPINDRIFT, by its very nature and substance constantly seeking out connections and attachments, spinning out sandy filaments of itself to join together its components and form one inimitable shape. Though itself technically a manmade island, the Cape has few real islands on either its inner or outer shores. The only true islands left are a handful found on the Cape's larger ponds, a half dozen or so in Pleasant Bay, the Elizabeths off Woods Hole, Washburn Island off Falmouth's south coast, and a few others in Buzzards Bay. Even the long finger of Monomoy Island, sometimes attached to the mainland, then lengthening, cut off, even cut in two, appears to be yearning outward to touch and connect the answering tip of Nantucket's Great Point.

WE LIVE IN A LAND OF LEISURELY LINKS with the human past. Each year the number of old houses and old natives shrinks. Old roads are straightened or obliterated. The oaks and pines grow up to original height and distribution, obscuring the stone walls running through former fields. The bogs return to cedar and maple swamp. The sea, as always, encroaches. The backyards in new subdivisions look more and more like part of the woods themselves. We and the land grow more prominent each day, and once again we find ourselves in original confrontation. The past is covered with leaves and buried, but what do we make of this, this other present, this waving, salutary, indifferent presence among us?

Chatham waterfront

Finger of sand on the flats

Rising tide covering a sandbar

THE OUTER BEACH

The high dunes of Truro

MAJESTIC AND MUTILATED, the great glacial scarp of Cape Cod's Outer Beach rises from the open Atlantic, separating it from Cape Cod Bay. Its many-colored sands and clays flow grain by grain, or in sudden shelving slabs, to replenish the shore below. The beach itself, broad and gently sloping in summer, short and steep in winter, arcs northward for over twenty miles, giving the walker a curved prospect two or three miles ahead at most. And always, coming onto the shore and reforming it, with measured cadences in calm weather, with life-destroying fury during northeast gales, is the sea. Here, as Henry Beston put it, "the ocean encounters the last defiant bulwark of two worlds." There is no other landscape like it anywhere.

WHEN I PULLED INTO NEWCOMB HOLLOW in Wellfleet, the beach was curiously empty. There were only three cars in the parking lot, and two of those left almost immediately. The waves were low and quiet, silently tossing massive logs and bright flags of sea lettuce about in the surf. A low fog was sitting on the beach like a cool shroud, though I could feel the hot sun, like a weight, beating down on it.

I walked north along the beach, my eyes smarting from a stiff, moist north wind. The first stretch of sand cliffs here is nearly completely barren of growth, partly from the constant foot traffic of the beach users. Farther on, the vegetation begins to reassert itself, climbing up the smooth slopes out of the wrack line. At the bottom were the stitched rows of beach grass, spreading by underground runners; then clumps of fleshy-leaved sea rocket, bristly sea-burdock, seaside goldenrod, and tufts of dusty miller with its lobed, pale-green leaves and long stalks of yellow flower clusters.

Beach figures in the distance proved to be improvised stick structures, erected and left on a previous summer's day. And though the footprints and vehicle tracks in the sand were so numerous that the beach in places resembled a railroad yard, I neither met nor saw another soul from Newcomb's Hollow to Brush Valley in Truro, nearly three miles away.

A dense fog continued to blow down the beach, shrouding visibility at both ends. The unexpected absence of people, and the desolate feeling of the fog, gave the impression of a mass exodus and brought to mind Thoreau's comment about this same beach, made nearly a century and a half ago, that "a thousand men could not have seriously interrupted it, but would have been lost in the vastness of the scenery as their footsteps in the sand." Even the Concord tourist's hyperbolic imagination, however, could not have envisioned the millions that would someday visit here, so that those same footsteps would actually threaten to alter the scenery; and yet, it seemed, a little moisture and sea breeze that day had blown them all away like sea foam and restored the beach to its ancient vastness and majesty.

As the cliffs began to rise over fifty feet above sea level, I left the beach, climbing up one of those diagonal foot trails cut into the face of the scarp— something like a mountain path, narrow and flat, and comparatively firm after the recent rain. Reaching the top, I continued on the path that runs along the crest just back from the edge. This path is, like the beach, both a permanent and ephemeral road, in this case manmade, but constantly forced to relocate as the cliffs recede from year to year.

The dips and rises of the crest, the fantastic topography, the occasional views of the receding beach, and the long, rolling vistas landward make this perhaps the most interesting stretch of bluffs to walk along the entire Outer Beach. Here is one place, at least, where the Cape's extremes are vertical as well as horizontal. The highest point of land on the Outer Cape is along this section, a summit marked on the U.S. Geological Survey maps as "Pamet," climbing a giddy one hundred seventy-seven feet above the beach (though this figure likely changes from year to year).

Yet everything is on the Cape's characteristically diminutive scale, so that I felt like a giant striding with a few steps from summit to summit along a sandy mountain range, complete with miniature peaks, cirques, bowls, and knife-edges. Every time the crest trail swung out to the edge, I peered over and startled a flock of gulls that were roosting on the slope, sending them out into the fog where they disappeared, reassembling farther north, where, later, I would start them again—a kind of larger version of the shepherding game one plays with flocks of shorebirds along the beach.

To the west I looked out over a vast and tilted plain of stunted vegetation. The drifting patches of fog both veiled its outlines and intensified a remarkable variety of greens: patches of poverty grass, carpets of bearberry, beach and upland grasses, thickets of beach rose, bayberry, and beach plum, bands of shiny scrub oak and dark pitch pine—surely one of the most distinctive and recognizable landscapes in the world.

At intervals the crest trail swung inland and joined a wider and more substantial jeep trail. Along its soft surface were numerous fresh tracks of deer that had apparently been coming in my direction, had scented or heard my approach, and had turned off the road. They were probably bedded down within yards of me

Cliff face, Outer Beach

Lobster buoy brought in by the surf

somewhere in the low, dark-green blanket of scrub oak, but I knew I could wait there all day and never see or hear a sign of them.

I strode, with my folded umbrella set across my shoulders like a yoke, across an open field of bright, rounded tufts of beach heather surrounded by tall, waving beach grass, among hardy stands of gnarled and weathered chokecherry, through thickets of beach plum with their hard green fruits already as large as marbles in this year of excellent berry sets. Their stiff twigs were entwined with numerous vines of wild grapes, all sprouting clusters of lime-green fruit as yet no bigger than grape seeds, glowing beneath the broad, arched grape leaves. How lush and thick and heavy with promise these eroding fragments of beach bluff can appear!

Shortly beyond the Pamet summit I descended to the beach again, staying on it until I reached a break in the cliff face at Brush Valley, a short distance south of Ballston Beach. As I walked up the hard narrow path of this ancient glacial valley (one of the few on the Outer Beach whose gradient, or slope, runs west to east), the uninterrupted hills of scrub oak rose sharp and huge into the fog. The screams of the invisible gulls loomed over me, dwarfing my presence. We need to be over-whelmed like this, on occasion, by some unpeopled expanse of the land where we live, even to fear it a little—that it goes on so long without us.

Went down to Nauset Beach about 2 p.m. today. Parking lot and beach deserted. I thought more would be there. Walked out to the beach where dune crest meets wave crest. Grass pale yellow like wheat waving over the ivory sand. Sea intense blue-green. White combers plowing in towards shore and churning up rainbow-colored spray like a thousand fountains. A few white gulls pacing unconcernedly down the beach. The waves sending up spray into a pale, blue sky that held a few soft lavender clouds, edged by the cold with pink. All was light and white—with one red soda can in the surf.

I WENT DOWN TO THE SHORE on New Year's Day, just before high tide on the morning following a furious northeaster. The storm itself had blown rapidly out to sea during the night, and the wind had careened around to the west, giving rise to a strange sight: a clear and sunlit beach on which the mighty surf, still in the throes of the storm and now approaching its flood, dashed itself in magnificent chaos.

Such a surf, swept back by the wind and etched in light, had passed through all stages of watery fury. No longer a series of breakers, it had become a shattering wall of green and white, crest breaking upon crest, wave receding crashing into wave oncoming. The sound it made was not a roar; it was more like a wind, a low, hollow, insidious whine that slowly grew in pitch and intensity, like the sound of a jet turbine accelerating, before it broke and dissolved into the next oncoming whine.

The air itself was full of the mist of its destruction, intersecting rainbows and flashes of light, and it smelled sweet, new-made, and wonderfully exhilarating. In no other place I know can you get so close to ultimate, unbridled force with so little risk as on the ocean shore.

AT NAUSET LIGHT the sea had a strange, restless look to it. The force of the offshore wind seemed to balance perfectly the landward movement of the swells, so that the resultant motion of the water expressed a restless indecision, as though it were about to burst forth into a new form or pattern. The breaking waves, with their tops sheared back in a potent spray, looked not so much like Homer's plunging horses as like dozens of whales strenuously beaching themselves, spouting as they went. But this was only the *image* they called up. The impression was really more of something being sheared, used up, disintegrated, like a piece of wood going through a shaper, much of its mass being transformed into a spray of sawdust.

When the forces of wind and sea interplay like this and work against one another, they seem to resolve themselves into a heightened formality of movement. Everything on them, even the little foolish fishing boats bobbing about far out on the moving surface, appears to move more slowly, and with great sureness and dignity, as in some ancient ritual. It gives the same impression as that of people of strong character, moving under great, controlled emotion. There is a little stiffness,

Sunrise and draggers

Sand-scoured driftwood

or unnaturalness, in the movements, outwardly, and only little fine resolutions escaping at the edges—as in swift shifts of the eyes, or little spasms at the fingertips—betray the volcanic forces beneath. The rest is a controlled madness.

THE OUTER BEACH LOSES HEADLAND each year, visibly reminding us that we live on a disappearing land, once again, in its gentle way, serving as a concentrated metaphor for the rest of it: a cooling earth, a dying star, a dissolving universe.

Yet we are also reminded by these very processes, by the bars that build, the spits that lengthen, the marshes and the embayments that silt in and fill up, that there may be more building going on than we know, that dissipating heat and disappearing matter may somewhere be caught by an interstellar wind of cosmic current, swept up and remade into new shores across a fathomless sea. I know too little physics to be sure such things are not happening.

I WAS ALONE ON THE BEACH that morning. The tide was low and the surf even lower, barely a surf at all, falling in lackadaisical one-foot waves as though it resented having to break at all. Recent storms had cut the summer berm of the upper beach in a sheer, short cliff nearly its entire length, forming a wavering line of sand palisades up to five feet high down the beach.

I went down to the edge of the tide, which was still going out, where a thin film of upwash, clear and foam-edged, slid over the small stones that were constantly milled and ground against one another at the bottom of the beach. The rounded stones had the color and the spotted pattern of tern eggs. From this point the dune slopes appeared heavily striated with dark, purplish, wind-blown deposits of magnetite, in the form of tall elongated S's. They looked, I thought, like the wave patterns on the side of a mackerel, or the pleats on the throat of a finback whale, or the corrugated sand ripples on the tidal flats, or . . .

Patterns, endlessly repeated patterns, of stone reflecting egg, egg reflecting dune, dune reflecting tide and wave, wave reflecting fish, and on and on, as though all life, and non-life as well, were imitating one another, or had risen from a very limited set of deep structures, or generating laws, expressed in a myriad of natural syntactical forms.

What were these laws? What makes everything on the beach fit together so? I have learned some of the answers, but in the face of its orchestrated reality they seem to explain nothing at all. Sometimes I think I walk these beaches as the old Cape Codders read their worn Bibles, tracing the same verses over and over, comforted, even mesmerized by their familiar sound and majestic cadences, yet always hoping to get at something further, some final meaning that is always offered and withdrawn, always just out of reach.

FRIDAY NOON I MANAGED TO SLIP OUT to the beach for a couple of hours. I drove north to the end of the pavement on the road north of Nauset Light. The cliffs were all white and rough-lipped from last night's snow and February's storm, except for where snow avalanches had torn away and rolled down onto a broad beach apron of snow below, leaving wide, ruddy scars on the face of the scarp like claw marks.

I walked north. On my right, a froth-scummed sea rolled about chaotically in post-storm fury. On the beach it was like walking along a slanted floor of a trough between descending walls. At one point I came to a section where the dwarf forest—mostly locusts, scrub oak, and cherry—grows along the edge of the bluffs—trees all less than twelve feet high. A raft of a half-dozen locusts had been dislodged and was sliding slowly down the cliff face like some strange floating island. I climbed up to examine it and found one of last summer's bird's nests still caught in the branches. Paused halfway down the cliff face, the marooned grove looked as if it had been cast up from the sea, thrown up upon the wall of the cliff by some giant wave. I wondered if it would leaf out one more time this spring, blossom in some last blind offering of white pendant flowers, a part of nature to the end, its allegiance to continuity unconditional upon the chances for success.

What a strange vision of life this beach presents! It is a continual going down to glory, a visual transformation and refunding of substance and process. No wonder fishermen cling so tenaciously to their impractical professions. On the beach there is nothing but a continuous immediate present of opportunity and risk, an ongoing casting out and hauling in, where all is sown and harvested in one throw, and nothing hangs upon contingencies.

The Outer Beach

Chatham fish pier

W E W E R E R E C E N T L Y V I S I T E D by some friends who moved from the Cape to Vermont several years ago. Their three young sons had been born off-Cape and had never seen the ocean. We took them all down to Nauset in the afternoon, where a heavy surf clawed away at the summer berm, creating a sharp shelf two feet high, while an offshore wind blew back the crests of the waves like a thousand horses' manes. The boys watched for several minutes in silent awe, until finally the eight year old turned to his father and asked, "Dad, when is it over?"

I T I S A F T E R E L E V E N N O W, and the fog has returned. The wind has once again become a steady south-southeast, and beyond the line of dunes I hear the imperative thumping of the ocean surf as it marches toward its full flood. Feeling restless, I place a Coleman lantern in the window as a beacon and set out across the dunes. I walk southeast, obliquely to the shore, following the sound of the surf. Sights and sounds both are muffled in the darkness and fog. Chatham Light is only an obscure, intermittent glow off to my right. From the unseen wet hollows in the dunes come the high, dry, toneless screams of Fowler's toads, sand-colored amphibians of the beaches that breed well into summer.

I seem to be traveling in a dim world of homogenized senses, where distance and dimension cease to exist. I walk for an indeterminate time without seeming to get any nearer to the beach, when all at once I smell it immediately ahead: a rich, salt-spiced nosegay of odors, redolent of growth and decay. Smell is often the sharpest sense on the beach at night, particularly at this time of year, when the salt marshes are "working," producing new crops of salt hay and cordgrass, and the exposed peat ledges and windrows of eelgrass warmed by the daytime sun give off their pungent fragrances.

The tide is approaching its high. The seethe of incoming foam laps and sloshes just below the wrack line on the upper beach, sliding back toward the dark breakers with a bubbly, sucking withdrawal. The breaking crest of the waves and the foamy swash edge appear to be outlined with a faint phosphorescence, but it is hard to tell in the obscurity of the fog. When I look down at the wrack line itself—a knotted tangle of rockweed, dulse, mermaid's tresses, broken claws, and discarded shells—it is speckled with thousands of pale, yellow-green bits of light, like coals scattered onto ice at night. These are the bioluminescent plankton, hordes of diatoms, dinoflagellates, and copepods that in summer often fill vast stretches of ocean with a cold biological glow, a sort of *aurora maritima*, so that ships plowing through these living shoals of light leave wide wakes of flickering fire behind them.

The schooner Hindu, *Provincetown*

Some of the larger glowing particles in the wrack line are hopping about, like sparks from resinous kindling. Shining my light on them, I see the bouncing forms of sand hoppers, also called beach fleas—miniature, shrimplike crustaceans about a third of an inch long with huge eyes and pearly white bodies. By day these creatures live in tiny burrows they dig at the upper edge of the shore, but at night they come out to feed on the tide's leavings. When they ingest the phosphorescent plankton, their semitransparent bodies begin to glow, like miniature jars full of fireflies. As I watch these strange, glowing creatures leaping about, I become aware of other lights on the beach. Three beach buggies loom out of the fog from the north, their headlight beams lurching drunkenly over the inner sand trail behind the dunes. As they pass by the cut to the beach where I stand, I can make out fishing poles strapped to their front fenders. One tries to cut out to the beach over a dune, fails, and roars back onto the track. They pass swiftly, their lights disappearing into the fog before them, and where they had been I hear the lovely, mournful, solitary note of the piping plover, a small, sand-colored shorebird that nests at the base of the dunes.

Usually I resent the intrusions of these machines on the beach, their meaningless lights and harsh sounds, but now I understand what drew them and I feel a strong urge to follow them down the dark beach down past the last cottages to the far tip of the spit where the sands perpetually shift and the night herons feed, where men cast their hooks into the curved breakers to pull living, flapping, cold fish-flesh out of the sea. We all have a desire to seek out such primal encounters, however clumsily or blindly. And the relentless complexity and growing numbers of our society seem to force us to seek them at ever odder hours and in ever stranger places, as on this exposed and shrouded beach, flooded and freshened by the night.

THE BURNING RITUAL
OF THE YEAR

Beach plums in blossom

THIS YEAR, WITH THE RIPENING of the first beach plums, I have another chance to run by outdoor clocks and calendars. This time, in the ripening and gathering of them, the beach plums seem part not just of the seasonal ambience, but of a larger fruit and berry cycle that stretches virtually unbroken around the trunk of the year, one in which I have, by bits and fragments, become deeply and unconsciously involved.

Beyond the plums, in still September, are the wild grapes, the hidden grapes, whose lush sweet fragrance, as palpable and elusive as the song of a woodthrush, steals out from under banks of green, overlapping grape leaves to overwhelm the nostrils. With the grapes, and easier to discover, are the Cape's wild apples, the warped, green, tart fruits that hang from a hundred wild apple trees along the main streets and in the overgrown fields of the town. Untended and largely ungathered, they drop one by one and, near the old gristmill, go bouncing and rolling down the pavement and into the pools of the herring run, where they bob and mix in the swirling currents, making their own autumn brew.

Beyond the grapes and apples of September stretch the wide, wine-colored cranberries of early October. There, in some sunny, sheltered, abandoned bog, we sit and gather a few quarts by hand on a lazy Sunday afternoon, while late dragonflies warm themselves on old shed walls and the World Series (always someone else's) plays itself out on the transistor nearby.

And beyond them, in November or early December, are the bayberries, best picked after the first frost. Down in the dune swales of the Provincelands or Sandy Neck, or out on some marsh island, wrapped now in hats and coats, we rub the gray waxy berries off the twigs between our palms, letting them fall into the buckets below. Myrtle warblers flit in and out of cover, as though to inquire who else is interested in their winter food supply, while swirling flakes of the year's first snowfall fly like moths at evening and begin to obscure an already obscure landscape. Though not an edible fruit, bayberries are gathered for their waxy coatings, as useful and necessary as the others, to bring fragrance and light inside at the candle-end of the year.

Even when winter closes its erratic and intermittent grip on the land in January, February, and March, there can still be found, poking up through the damp snow or scattered throughout the bare, pasted leaf-floor of the oak woods, the bright red fruits of the wintergreen, or checkerberry. Each of these diminutive woodland plants holds its pea-sized berry dangling solitary among dark, shiny, leathery leaves—glowing bits of unexpected life with a Lifesaver taste, to be picked and tasted sparely along the paths and game trails of a dead season.

And then, just as the last checkerberries dry and wither and the alewives start up the thawing creeks, shadbush bursts out in low, leafless clouds of white blossoms along the roadsides and stream banks. The fruit of the shadbush matures fast, and within a few weeks becomes the first edible fruit of the new season. Though widely picked in the South, where it is known as sarvissberry, the shadberry is rarely gathered here anymore. But for those who know it, it provides a tart and tasty treat even before the first strawberries arrive in June.

With strawberries I cannot pretend to be a wild gatherer, for the local crop of wild strawberries is admittedly meager. Instead, in early June, I drive over to the eastern part of our town where Russell Jenkins, a physics major from Williams College with a boy's enthusiasm for applying new techniques to old tasks, has carved out a thriving, pick-your-own strawberry farm. I pick these thick, oversized, lusciously sweet, cultivated fruits with scores of other carefully regulated patrons in endless lines of irrigated and fertilized rows; yet these berries nonetheless seem as integral with the land and passing seasons as their wild cousins. Certainly, surrounded as it is with a growing monotony of "unique" condominium developments and "exclusive planned living communities," this farm represents an unconventional and individual enterprise that flies in the face of prevailing land-use philosophy, and so is itself as wild and as radical as any native fruit. At any rate, these fields, which only a few winters ago were pine and briar, have been made to sing berries in rich red notes along staves of green rows, and for two or three weeks in early summer we all get to join in the chorus.

As the strawberry flood subsides, the heat of July brings on the high- and low-bush blueberry season, as variable and unpredictable a harvest as scallops. A good set of fruit in May can be thick and promising, but a prolonged drought in June can result in a shriveled and disappointing crop. I usually go after the less-sought-after but more dependable huckleberries, ubiquitous and darkly succulent throughout our deciduous woods. Later still, there are raspberries and blackberries, cooking in the August sun on long, menacing, curved blue stems. And all the time, through the long soft summer, under the dust of roadsides or high along the crests of salt- and wind-washed dunes, the miniature marble-globes of beach plums are slowing growing and gathering to themselves the colors of autumn.

I have, of course, left many berries and other fruits out of this account that are not on my personal list, but which others will know. Furthermore, this berry cycle is only one of many offered throughout the year here. There are fish cycles, crab cycles, shellfish cycles, and waterfowl cycles. And beyond such strictly "useful" native plant and animal crops, there are uncounted other cycles: songbird cycles,

Beach rose hip

frog cycles, butterfly cycles, flower cycles, or simply the marvelous progression of a single maple tree in one's own yard through the months of the year.

What is striking about all these cycles is the availability for participation they still afford. Modernized, suburbanized, overoccupied as this land surely has become, the list of near-to-hand entrances into the ancient rhythms of natural life remains almost endless. And all, of course, are ultimately parts of that great cycle of the sun which, like a revolving carnival Roundup, gathers us all—berries, fish, clams, birds, and people alike—into its great, star-flinted wheel.

SPRING HAS TAKEN POSSESSION OF THE CAPE this week, though the *signs* of it are still few. Temperatures stay up above forty at night, the wind roars like a black river around the house, and the moon sails higher, fuller, and later each night through the bedroom window. Yesterday's warmth dried up last weekend's late snow almost completely except on the southwest slopes of Berry's Hole, where the beeches, flinging up their branches in frenzied adoration (like the hair of wild women), still stand rooted in white skirts. The snow waters the earth in rivulets. At the bottom of the hole the last of the old ice lies under a half foot of new meltwater, yellowed and rotten like moldy cheese. The water is as sweet and clear as bogwater is ever likely to be. Still nothing moves on it but the fingers of the wind.

THE FIRST TERN OF THE SEASON came flying up the beach at me as though shot from a sling: a cleaving, twisting, sharp-edged blur, so that I instinctively ducked as it passed swiftly overhead and was gone. Rarely am I challenged so directly by these birds outside of their nesting colonies, but the first tern is always an event here—like the first alewife or woodcock—in some ways more eagerly awaited since these birds' foothold on the spits and barrier islands where they nest has always been tenuous and precarious at best.

This was early in May, on Barnstable's Sandy Neck, and as I walked down that cobbly beach, listening to the sucking waves of an ebbing tide rattling the stones together, I thought how much the face of these waters had changed in the past few weeks. In winter we turn away from its fierce, blue-gray sterility to whatever comfort the pine woods could offer. Now they appeared as wide, lush fields, deep green and clear in complexion, so that once again we look to the sea for fertility and renewal.

Common terns

Stony Brook herring run, Brewster

New currents had widened the beach, making it a pathway again for men and for birds. Shimmering, orange-breasted barn swallows raced along its edges, cleaving the air in parabolic cuts, harvesting invisible flying insects. In a shallow inlet two laughing gulls, handsome black-headed birds slightly larger than the terns, paddled and dabbled for food in the pools, undisturbed by my presence. As I passed they paused in their feeding, turned and faced each other, and cackled hoarsely.

Above the waters, confirming the promise of its new colors, I now saw more common terns, distinguishable from other tern species here by their short tails, black-tipped red bills, and characteristic harsh *kee'-arr* calls. They wheeled fifty feet and more above the surface of the Bay, dive-bombing down into and below the water for several seconds, rising again with small, slender fish held horizontally in their sharp bills. The sun was shining with a hurt brilliance on sand and water, but the wind was still rough and the early couples on the beach huddled together in sand hollows under blankets and in sleeping bags. Of all the things I saw that morning only the first tern was alone, and it appeared to be hurrying toward something.

Y ESTERDAY NOON, COMING UP THE SLOPE behind Mrs. Scott's house, I suddenly found myself face to face with an enormous stand of beach plum in full flower. It was, in a fresh sense, spectacular, and was like standing in front of the petrified burst of spray from a giant breaker. Not quite petrified, though, for the perfect white blossoms, swaying gently like a woman's breasts, were alive with the swarming and low hum of hundreds of bees: large, yellow and black bumblebees, their leg sacs heavy with beige-colored bags of pollen; domestic honey bees; and smaller wild bees, with some yellow on them and black, pointed abdomens.

Though I waded into the stand and they buzzed on all sides of me, they did not seem to notice my presence, but worked smoothly and methodically from one blossom to another, as in some well-coordinated dance. No functionless beauty could equal it.

PINE POLLEN WEEK. A constant drift of it, like saffron fog, dusts cars and decks, collects in rain puddles, washes up in broad, yellow-green ribbons against the pond shores. This blind blanket of fertility is a prime example of nature's strategy of oversowing. Under the microscope the individual grains appear as irregular, light-golden spheres, angular without detail, like chunks of rain, a bit less than one-tenth of a millimeter across. Pine pollen is supposedly extremely rich in nutrients. A botanist friend tells me that young spiders eat their webs in order to gain the protein from the pollen caught in them. On mornings this time of the year one spots spiderwebs as easily as after a heavy dew. They look like veils of yellow paint.

COOL AND BREEZY TODAY after several muggy-buggy days. There is nothing so rich as these brilliant, cool, stirred-up days in June. The wind rises up under the rug of the land, turning over the season late out here, amid the sluggish, reluctant ocean. The trees in their leaves' fullness are pressed down, rushing and thrashing with the wind's desire. I try to read outside, and the interplay of white, sunlit brilliance and deep, dappled shade sweeps my eyes off the page.

Writing here on the deck, I watch the wind lift and shake out the new green carpet. Just now a curious thing fell out of the sky onto the back of my hand: a small, empty shell of some insect, barely an eighth of an inch long, light transparent yellow-brown, like the case of a horseshoe crab, wingless, with black eye-dots and pointed appendages. It reminds me of some crab zooea—a bit of weightless detritus, or terrestrial plankton, from the rich restless ocean of air around me.

JUNE SEEMS PARTICULARLY LUSH this year, moving heavily through itself with leaves and soft winds. The other day my daughter came home from school and said, "What a *green* day!" From the bedroom window the two dimensional sunset-silhouetted maze of black trunks and branches has become a labyrinth of vaulted and convoluted passageways, tunnels, pockets, and recesses, filtering the dust of the sun's gold through its green chambers, creating dreams of sculptured space and tesselated floors, and a deep desire to walk and thread ourselves through its intricate depths.

Marshmallow blossoms

Sea lavender in bloom

SUMMER DOLDRUMS. If you don't watch out they can be infectious. The roads are clogged and traffic slows to a halt. The blood too becomes thick and sluggish. The limbs grow heavy and droop like the boughs beginning to labor under ripening fruit. The eye begins to glaze over with a dull film, like the mats of algae growth covering the bogs. And even the mind feels itself slowly eaten away, like the roadside leaves, with rot and insects.

Whenever I begin to feel this way, when August begins to hang heavy and hot on my heart, I know it is time to get to the beach again, where even on the deadest days there is some small wind blowing—time to go down to the Bay's blue waters, to shoulder past the sodden and sulking crowds plastered with sand, past the crackerbox cottages swamped with roses, to herd small flocks of sanderlings and plovers along the water's edge, to gather sprays of sea lavender, to be lifted by a dark shield of bugling geese rising across the green, sharp-bladed marshes, to plunge at last into a deep tidal creek, losing myself in its strong, out-running currents, tumbling head over head with the crab shells and the pebbles, carried swiftly toward the Bay until I bottom out on clean, white sand.

NATURE'S SUMMER ENDS before ours does. The shorebirds and the sea lavender tell me that even when my world seems to have come to a sodden halt, others are already in motion. The stiff-branched, bell-like heads of sea lavender, or marsh rosemary, dot the upper borders of the marsh. Their diminutive purple flowers bloom with the arrival of the first shorebirds and have always been to me a sign of summer's ending. They are the earliest of the fall flowers and the loveliest of marsh plants, long gathered and dried for a winter's remembrance. The flower stalks are surrounded by basal rosettes of rounded, spatulate leaves, already turning brown and dark-red. The sprays form lavender veils through which I gaze and watch sand crickets, beach ants, and other small lives scurry.

WE HAVE HAD MAGNIFICENT FALL WEATHER the past several days, ushered in by Hurricane David's departure on Friday. At night the air is cool and clear, the leaves seem annealed with moonlight, the edges of dark tree shadows vibrate on the brilliant grass. One drives and walks through the suddenly empty streets as through a wilderness of sun and shadow. The sun backlights strong dramatic

The Brewster Store

Old house, Yarmouthport

Dunes and storm front

assemblies of clouds. There is no counterpart to this in the vernal sun. All is centrifugal and coming apart then. There is movement, too, in autumn, but it is a settled, composed movement. Things have a certain grandeur, and nobility, eschewing the wild rush, the cataracting passions of spring. Everything is fully separate in the clear, distinguishing light—the clouds, the bending, heavy trees. The pumpkins swell and turn orange in the long grass, the sunflower droops and covers her heavy, seedful head with dark, lapping leaves, the sea pumps against the summer berm in strong, measured swells. Everything drops, bends, sways, falls in fruition.

U NLIKE NEW ENGLAND'S MORE NORTHERN DISPLAYS that wash down out of the hills and ridges, the Cape's autumn colors tend to well up out of our wetlands. Swamp azaleas give ruddy borders to our ponds and swamp maples ring them with yellow, peach, and deep scarlet. The color spreads gradually into the surrounding upland, infusing it with the subdued hues of huckleberry and bayberry, the brighter colors of sumac and blueberry, up to the red banners of poison ivy and Virginia creeper waving from our pines and telephone poles.

By late summer, the salt marshes are already tinged with yellow, and dotted here and there with the shy, pale patches of sea lavender, one of the many late-blooming marsh flowers. Now the spartina grasses cover the marshes with a rich tawny coat, like a lion's mane, and wide patches of sea-blite and marsh samphire glow like coals. On these clear autumn days the ponds and bays take on an intense cobalt blue seen only at this season.

On the outer beaches I sense a further, final going forth of the season. The tenacious beach grass lifts its wheat-like seed stalks into the chill air; the salt spray rose sports both its large red hips and some late blossoms; the beach plums drop their withered purple fruits into the sand, and seaside goldenrod waves its yellow plumes above the dunes. The shorebirds, too, are almost gone, but out on the flats, digging some quahogs, I am periodically buzzed by flocks of common terns, skimming low over the water like fighter planes. These world travelers are now massing in groups in preparation for their long flights south. I look at them carefully, knowing it will be seven months until they return.

More than any one occurrence, however, the most pervasive change of the season here is one of light. It is a clear light, a light that intensifies colors and etches shapes. It is a constant light, a low slanting light, a morning light, all day long.

The softest, brightest days come in November. The color is all low now, but as delicate and lovely as April's pastels. October's blaze of foliage is gone, but there is still wine and vermilion on the huckleberry and blueberry bushes, and the viburnum leaves illuminate the woods with a pale, almost trembling light.

Out on the salt marshes the long slanting light of late fall intensifies the variety of hues. Tall stands of phragmites reed guard the upper marsh borders, waving their feathery seed heads. Cowlicks of salt hay tumble like tawny waves across the broad peat meadows. Along the water's edge, bent stalks of cord grass are washed by the gentle undulations of a silky, oily sea; with each roll of the tide the thin stems are wetted and glint like strands of polished copper.

By mid-November the creeping cranberry vines have turned the bogs into a patchwork quilt of deep wine-reds and purples, dark colors that gather all the warmth of the low sun to themselves and seem to glow. A few late, pale-lemon butterflies wander across the bogs, wheeling upward in pairs around a shifting invisible center, like earths and moons.

MONDAY'S LIGHT, simple and intense, abstracted the landscape, outlining fields, yards, porches, roofs, and fences with an almost visible edge. The leaves are almost gone, but for a few full surging heads of maples and beeches. The spare clean colors of the New England houses—red on yellow, blue on white—glow with an atavistic intensity, transforming and revealing them as something archetypal, so that the absence of any human figure, without or within, is appropriate. The full illumination of a westering sun is set off by banks of dark, bluish-gray clouds to the east, tinged with pink at their crests. Such light, such autumnal light, makes forms at once eternal and ephemeral. It is the light of the season, the light of immolation.

EACH SEASON HERE CREATES its own perspective and dictates the way we see it. Winter blows us briskly along a thoroughly hardened beach; we slip along the frozen sand, unable to find a foothold. Winter forces us to keep moving, to take in the landscape in sweeps and glances of the eye, large bracing gulpfuls, major outlines only. Most senses are muffled. In this sharpest of seasons details escape us.

We are like the Bay itself, its urgent lappings stilled and matted with slush ice and dark, crushing seaweed. Our narrowed vision abstracts the landscape into essentials: large chunks of pack ice littering the beach, a wide gray shield of water beyond, and in the distance a thin line of brant—and that is all.

I pass quickly a naked, ice-edged ditch that strikes memory. I recall where last summer I had crept softly there beneath a thick, concealing canopy of shrubs and bushes, knelt first, and then lay down at full length beside the languid, moss-lined stream. I think I stayed there a season, watching luxurious underwater weeds lengthen and weave their fantastic patterns while delicate surface insects traced their soft designs: listening to hidden birds, thrushes and warblers, pipe gently; and waiting carefully for the secret of that slow stream to glide gently toward me. Now it is all gone, like a dream; the dark slit of half-frozen water slides swift and barren along the edge of my memory as I hurry by in the opposite direction.

And yet, just as we begin to get winter into our bones, setting our teeth to greet it head on, it goes. The wind shifts to the southwest, a line storm rushes in and sweeps the Cape viciously for an hour, spitting hail and cracking lightning. The temperature rises twenty degrees in two hours and a warm, wet rain settles down upon us. For two nights it pours and pours out of the southeast and the snow goes in a flush, leaving only crumpled, forlorn patches.

There is a letting go of the frozen earth: driveways become deep mires, leaves are matted down with heavy, wet weight, and everything looks strangely bare again. From the saturated ground a dampness slowly rises and permeates the air, giving it an underwater quality. From the woods below the house I hear strange, choking frog calls. Even the squirrels, chattering in the trees, sound tropical and aquatic.

For a few days the earth steams, springlike, teasing sixty. Some chickadees and a cardinal venture a few spring calls. Spears of chard poke up green and bright from the ruins of our garden, and pussy willows bloom in Chatham. By the barren ditch I find a few soft sprays of delicate new fern fronds. Mallards and coots return to the ponds, and harbor seals are seen moving back into the unlocked marsh inlets. By the next weekend the wind turns round again, temperatures plummet, and four inches of new snow arrive.

How are we to live in such a place, in such changeable seasons? Winter is a series of daily events, turning with the tide, with the wind, allowing us no extended sweeps of rigidity. It is the most various of our seasons. In its grip this thin crescent of land swings like a crazy pendulum, dragging us back and forth between

Early spring snowstorm

extremes of weather. It is a great outdoor drama; but to appreciate it requires a constant alertness and adjustment of mood to its changes. Otherwise we are merely swept along in its currents or live by the calendar only, blotting the season itself out of our minds.

A LIGHT SNOW THIS MORNING, slightly more than half an inch and stopping by 8:30—one of the earliest I remember here. It coats the apple leaves still on the trees. It spreads out on fallen pine needles and grass blades like ice crystals spreading out onto a pond, or threads of white mold creeping over the yard. It turns the garden marigolds into bouquets of white mums.

There is a strong and characteristic feeling about the first snowfall of the year. It brings us into the new year with a nostalgic shock. Even on the cloudiest of days there is a glare and a brightness to it. It makes us feel slightly ill, but in a pleasantly recuperative way. We are at once more vulnerable and unclothed to the open universe. It is a bit like going to heaven; everything is at once strange, yet familiar. It breaks down the enclosed present, opening us up to the white stretches of eternity. The wood paths that appear in the snow are full of ghosts. There was a finality this morning when Beth left for work and Katy left for school, as if I might never see them again. They went off, and were swallowed up by the white whale. All this from a few centimeters of semi-congealed precipitation.

S NOW, SNOW, SNOW. A white weekend: a blanket of five inches Friday night, another two or three today. It makes the local headlines: "Freak Storm Batters Cape." It comes out through the radio and we eat it for breakfast, curse the inconvenience, and drive nails deeper into the coffins of our childhood.

Despite the histrionic headlines and Chamber of Commerce protestations, such ocean snowstorms are not "freak," but infrequently regular here, glazing our narrow land with white and leaving the mainland barren. I would like to see the Cape from a satellite after such a winter blow; it must look like a long, curled, ivory tusk thrusting out from the darker mainland, a horn on which many a winter's ship has impaled itself.

Winter in the woods

Thursday the temperature dropped fifteen degrees during the afternoon. That night the wind howled with a hollow dry whine. It was six degrees when we went to bed, two below in the morning. The sun glinted on the snow like sand. The yard was littered with snapped twigs and pine needles, burned off in the night. Every footstep and depression held a pocketful of newly fallen oak leaves, stubborn since October, and still curled like coppery claws. The wind, a night mason, had formed miniature dune ridges of snow in the yard, and along the roadsides had shaped the drifts with a horizontal ridge, like chimney caps.

Four inches of soft snow fell last night, making a world of stag antlers in the woods in the morning. Late this afternoon, in the pink pre-glow of sunset, I climb to the roof and shovel off the solar panels, then come down and walk out through the virgin snow of the yard down into Berry's Hole. The toboggan run is a white tunnel, uterine. At the bottom of the bowl the maple limbs have been bowed down with snow. They dip into the black water where mushy ice is beginning to harden its bite. I am almost entirely enclosed by a dome of white, inside the shell of some fantastic, confectionery Fabergé egg. Everything is as still and silent as an artificial world. There is absolutely no sound or sign of moving life other than my own. The textures are those of an electron microscope print: abstract and sharp, compressed and foreshortened, as though I beheld fundamental alien structures, related to, but not of this world or dimension. Then, part way up the hill, the silence is broken by one small, somewhat querulous and tentative bird sound, a chirp really, as of something just hatched. It sounds like the beginning of the world.

The Inner Cape

Horse barn, Harwich

THE FARM STARES the late twentieth century straight in the eye. The exit road off the freeway leads right up to its front gate. From the gate one can hear the busy traffic whizzing along the highway, and overhead, the sudden sucking roars and sonic booms of invisible fighter jets from nearby Otis Air Force Base crashing through the skies.

I came upon it one autumn day as I was bicycling north from West Falmouth, pedaling hard against a prediction of heavy rains that afternoon, when my eye was caught by a familiar matrix of elements on the lefthand side of the road.

An old stone wall bordered the highway, setting off what lay on the other side like a footlight cover on an old stage. Beyond the wall an uncut field sloped steeply down to a small kettle pond rimmed with tupelos and maples. Further along the pond shore more stone walls climbed up out of the kettle hole to the top of the north rim, where there sat an ancient, porchless, two-story eighteenth-century farmhouse and detached barn. Beyond the buildings stretched a large level field with some small horses or ponies grazing in it.

It was one of those lovely, typical New England farmscapes that are now anything but typical—in fact, all but extinct—here on the Cape. So strongly did it seem to epitomize all the old small-scale farms that used to dot this region that I thought that must explain the strong sense of familiarity I felt upon seeing it, since I had never actually seen this particular farm before.

I had happened on it at a rather inconvenient time. My car was still fifteen miles away and the weather was looking more doubtful each minute. Still, it evoked a deep connection somewhere, something I could not immediately fathom. This old farm, a place I had never been to, called to me strongly as though out of memory itself. I got off the bike and wheeled it up the narrow paved drive.

A dead elm leaned precariously out over the driveway. One large limb hung suspended over the power line coming to the house, threatening to cut off its only visible link to the outside world. I stepped up to the ivy-covered doorstone and knocked, but there seemed to be no one about. Around the back of the house was a small attached porch. Screwed into its weathered floor planks was an old boot-scraper made from two horseshoes which served as ends and were welded together with steel straps. It was rusted and the brush bristles attached to each end had been worn down to nothing with use.

I stepped through a wooden gate and walked down toward the pond through the tilting front field overgrown with milkweed, uncut grass, chicory, and golden-rod. The grass rustled and clicked with waves of gray mottled grasshoppers that leaped before me. Down near the pond a bright male kestrel sat in a young maple

West Barnstable farm

tree. It suddenly leaped into the air, snatched a small yellow butterfly that was wandering over the grass, returned to its perch, and bent down to eat.

The pond, though small, was clear. I suspect it is fairly deep. On its waters floated small scarlet leaves, dropped from the massive tupelos that line its banks. I made my way up out of the pond bowl past a ragged series of deserted outbuildings, chicken coops, and a toolshed. All were covered with wild bittersweet vines just beginning to unpeel their brilliant autumn fruit.

The back section of the farm, which encompasses some forty acres, is a large, level pasture, kept cropped that afternoon by three tethered ponies—a white, a black, and a pinto. The pinto looked like she was wearing a coonskin cap until I realized that her front mane was completely matted with beggars' ticks picked up from the field while grazing. The horses looked up at me as I passed, rubbing hind legs alternately, flicking their long tails and tossing their heads nervously, weaving from side to side. They reminded me of small boats rocking against their moorings in a light wind.

I skirted the back edge of the farm, which is cut across by railroad tracks, and returned along the north side of the pasture. The grass was dotted with bright pink clover blossoms and numerous small white composites. A meadowlark rose up out of the grass on whirring wings, hovered a moment, then dropped and disappeared again. I wished I had been there to hear him sing in the spring. Meadowlarks have become less and less common on the Cape as their field habitat continues to disappear under the twin forces of development and reforestation, and they are a rare sight now.

Along the stone wall sat one of the rusted junk cars that seem to grow like pumpkins in the back corners of all old farms. A little farther along was a stack of enormous old timbers, perhaps dismantled from an earlier structure and piled here for use in a new project never started and now long forgotten. A woodchuck had now made his den beneath it. I saw his warm brown form lope through the grass and disappear as I approached. Some tenants are always indifferent to a change in ownership.

Coming back into the dooryard of the farmhouse I peeked into the open door of the large square barn. It was empty of livestock but full of that unmistakable pungent barn smell, a mixture of sweet hay and ammonia. As the strong raw odor washed over me, I suddenly realized what had drawn me so strongly to this farm that day. The barn smell released a flood of vivid tactile and sensory memories of another Cape farm I had known when I was in college, one at the other end of the peninsula and about the size of this one, where I had once spent a summer haying.

I remembered lifting the heavy, itchy, scented bales up onto the tractor-drawn wagon and stacking them high up into the hot, oven-dark August hayloft. I remembered riding its horses in the cool evenings, sometimes taking one into a nearby sailing camp to the wonderment of blond city boys. I remembered one stormy Halloween night when the power had been knocked out, watching the bloody birth of a calf in the glare of jeep headlights drawn up into the barn.

It had been the last working farm in that Lower Cape town, and there were many of us who loved it, who worked on it during the summers. The motivation was as much, if not more, the close contact it gave us with the earth and its animals as the low wages we got for our exhausting labor. It gave each of us our own set of indelible memories, and we flattered ourselves with myths we invented about its richness and immortality. The loam, we said, was six feet deep. The title, we said, was protected by a centuries-old land trust that would never allow it to be developed. It was simply too good a place and the people who ran it were simply too nice ever to disappear.

We were wrong, of course. Reality replaced myth as we grew older. The son who had intended to carry on the farm was killed in a highway accident. The old couple, unable to manage the farm by themselves, sold off the cattle and the pigs and eventually died. When the grandchildren grew up, some of them tried to maintain it as a horse stable, but zoning difficulties and sharply rising land values forced them to sell it to a developer in the end.

And then one day the bulldozers came in and cut out the new roads through the fields in which we had labored and ridden, revealing both the poor, stony subsoil and the all-too-ordinary vulnerability our farm shared with the rest of the Cape, and so at last made believers of us all.

As I pedaled out of the drive and headed north toward my car and shelter, the elm still leaned threateningly across the overhead wires. The field and the wind stirred, sending up milkweed seeds in wild flight from the grass. The ponies whinnied nervously in the far pastures, sensing the coming rain. In the near distance the public future, as represented by military aircraft and state highways, roared on. And the old house and the barn waited, as they had for more than two centuries, to weather out another storm.

Near the Truro–Wellfleet border, I struck off west through the woods toward Newcomb Hollow and came to an unpaved section of the Old King's Highway, originally laid out in 1660. At this point the old colonial road is no more than a narrow dirt cartpath running through shady and quiet woods, indistinguishable from any of the other wood roads that labyrinth their way through this section of Wellfleet. Only a few small eighteenth-century houses along its length suggest that this out-of-the-way dirt track was once the major thoroughfare down-Cape.

To the east I began to hear music. The secluded pine woods rippled and hummed with the muted and overlapping sounds of drums, cornets, mandolins, guitars, and stereos. They came from a scattered, extensive community of summer cottages, most of them older ones predating the National Seashore, which were strung out around the ponds at the head of the Herring River and along a bewildering complex of sand roads. The varying and broken strands of music that filtered through the afternoon air had an informal, lackadaisical quality to them, starting and stopping in mid-phrase, like birdsong.

In their haphazard rhythms and snatches of melody I sense the strong role that these woods and the houses they hide play for their seasonal inhabitants, a role which they can never play for one who, like myself, lives here year round. It must be for them a place out of their accustomed life, removed from its resigned and inexorable flow, a locale of wide margins where, for a weekend, two weeks, a month, or a season, they can still be who they once dreamed they were, lost in a maze of unregulated soft dirt roads, identified only by some rough wooden sign tacked to a pine trunk at an unnamed intersection in the woods, relaxing and making tentative music for its own sake, music that echoed anonymously back and forth across the waters that separated them.

The Buzzards Bay Moraine is the highest, hilliest, and rockiest of the three glacial moraines, or strings of low hills, that form the "backbone" of Cape Cod. Made up largely of chunks of granite that were dragged eastward off the mainland a hundred centuries ago by the Buzzards Bay Lobe of the great Wisconsin Stage Glacier, the hills of this moraine, stretching from the Cape Cod Canal bridge at Bourne on the north, southward to Woods Hole (and to the Elizabeth Islands beyond), contain more large boulders than any other area on the Cape. It is here, more than anywhere else on this shifting, changing piece of land, that one can get

Beebe Woods, Falmouth

a feeling of stability and solidity, of being inland instead of being forty miles at sea.

Covered with a hard, clayey soil and carpeted with a thick forest of oak, pine, and beech, these woods create a feeling of peace and calm, a sense of persisting forms. The hills and boulders are fossils of a vast glacial flow whose massive icy head traveled three thousand miles south from the Labrador Canadian Shield, planing and leveling with immense forces the once towering Appalachian mountain chain to leave its mark here as a terminal ridge of rock and glacial till. The woods are solid, firm, unyielding, and comparatively immobile. Here energy is held captive, molded into form; the trees themselves are living fossils of sunlight, air, and water, trapped into rigid, unmoving shapes that slowly spread their canopies and extend root systems to bind the hills and ravines into even more enduring shapes.

By late spring the leaves are out in full and the bird population, though large, is more often heard than seen. The muted calls of mourning doves, titmice, ovenbirds, towhees, chipping sparrows, cardinals, yellow warblers, chickadees, flickers, goldfinches, quail, redwings, and nuthatches filter thriough the fresh new greenery and perennial latticework of branches, and the drumming of a male grouse on his courting ground booms faintly like disappearing thunder somewhere in the distance.

Among the trees motion is, for the most part, furtive and unseen, or at a pace below human perception. A solitary swallow darts silently across the calm surface of a deep kettle pond. White may-stars, or star-flowers, flicker dimly in the dark undergrowth. The soft pink and white clusters of arbutus bloom briefly for a few weeks among the fallen leaves, but by the first of June they are brown and dry. The sharp, sudden call of a female redwing rings out once, and then is gone. Woods accomplish their business quietly, for the most part. In such a place the mind collects itself and imagines permanence.

In EARLY OCTOBER I RETURNED to the woods on a beautiful, crisp, clear autumn morning. Swallowed by the forest, I once again felt its hushed richness. The lady's slippers and mayflowers of late spring had been replaced by blue and orange woodland asters and the red berries of wintergreen. The earthy colors of the mushrooms dotted the forest floor. Oak leaves glowed with a subdued brilliance. Beeches curled their leaves into coppery scrolls, and their smooth trunks sported a variety of blue, green, and gray lichens. Beside the roadbed, bright green mats of hairycap moss and delicate fronds of maidenhair fern greeted the eye.

Swamp maple leaf

Barclay Pond, Chatham

At one bend in the road two large old pine trunks, felled by some forgotten storm, perhaps the famous hurricane of 1938, lay together in stranded majesty like huge twin skeletons of beached whales. They had, in fact, the color and crumbly texture of old whale bones found on the beach. Their long spires, still intact and lichen-encrusted, pointed due northeast, recording like frozen weathervanes the fate that rushed in from the southeast to fell them many years ago. Though it had not rained for nearly a week, several small puddles remained along the trail, attesting to the clayey base of the soil. Shallow and muddy, they nonetheless harbored several green frogs, somewhat sluggish in the cool October air, but still slippery enough to escape my grasp and come bobbing up again like emeralds, gold-rimmed eyes blinking. So life leaps at you where you least expect it.

The spring concert of birds had been whittled down to an astringent chorus of a few nuthatches, chickadees, some newly arrived pine siskins, and the constant, ready background of fall crickets. This time I noted that there is much sassafras in the undergrowth, along with huckleberry, highbush blueberry, and catbriar.

There is a richness to these moist autumn woods and a pungent odor of fecundity like that of a plowed field or a salt marsh when it begins to "work" in the spring. For in deciduous woods, the process of breakdown and decay is as important and as life-giving as spring growth. The decomposing bacteria and fungi that lie silent and unseen below the leaf layer are as much a part of the cycle of death and renewal as the visible leaves and singing birds, and far, far more numerous.

THE KETTLE PONDS OF NICKERSON STATE PARK contain some of the largest, deepest, and clearest waters on the peninsula, with clean sandy bottoms and shores ringed with stones and boulders that have been scoured from their bottoms and culled from their banks by millennia of storms, wind, and ice.

Clustered around its larger ponds—Cliff, Flax, Higgins—are many smaller ponds and bogs—shallower, eutrophic, full of pond lilies and frogs—that one stumbles on with sweet surprise. These are the geologic progeny of the main water bodies, and were once coves of the larger ponds. Some are still seasonally connected to them in high-water years. The sandy bars that now separate these side ponds from the main ones were created by the ponds themselves through a process that seems a miniature mimicry of similar processes along our ocean shores. Just as storm waves tear material from the cliffs and dunes of the Outer Beach, Cape Cod Bay, and Nantucket Sound, building up such large sand spits as

Cape Cod mosses and lichens

Cliff Pond, Nickerson State Park

Monomoy Island, the Provincelands, Nauset Beach, and Sandy Neck, so these ponds, whipped into miniature seas by fall and winter storms, wear away their bordering hills slowly and carry the material to form these smaller bars and spits. Eventually the bars completely cut off some of the coves and, without further access to the cleansing actions of the larger ponds, their aging process is usually hastened. Cliff Pond, largest of the Nickerson lakes, is surrounded like a hen with chicks by seven or eight of these little side waters in various stages of aging, and the process has not ceased.

You will not find ponds like these in the southern outwash plain of the Cape, nor in the wind-drifted sand hills of Provincetown. These are true kettle ponds, formed when the ice of the last Wisconsin Stage glacier stopped halfway across the present east-west section of the Cape, breaking off large chunks of ice which remained when the main ice sheet finally retreated some twelve thousand years ago. These chunks were subsequently buried by the till and rubble dropped by the retreating glacier. When they finally melted as well, the land above them sank into "kettle holes," creating these classic ponds.

It is their Arctic origin that accounts for their depth, their clarity and, I like to think, their coolness as well. Since their formation over ten millennia ago, the pond waters have no doubt undergone numerous recyclings by evaporation, ground seepage, and replenishment by rain at least as thorough as the complete replacement of the cells in my body which, I am told, takes place every seven years or so. Yet just as an invisible genetic code maintains my basic personality intact through all its physiological metamorphoses, so I seem to sense, cupping these clear pond waters in my hands, some lingering taste of their Labrador beginnings transmitted over the intervening ages.

WE NEED OUR PONDS HERE. A sea-girt land like this with no inland waters would be unendurable. They are our points of reference, our water compasses, pools of peace amid the unimaginable and constant flux of the ocean. We need, not simply solid land, but something to reflect the liquid pulse and beat of our own blood, something to rest our psyches in. The tide, you might say, is the ocean's obvious pulse, the flood and recession of the earth's waters. But who, riding the ocean's back, could credit it? Who could believe that the stately approach and withdrawal of the sea at the edges of our land had anything to do with the chaotic presence beneath him? No, we need our ponds to stay our restless souls on, ponds and

Swans on Mud Pond, East Dennis

the gentle pulse of the two-hearted tidal rivers veining our marshes. The ponds, too, have a pulse, slower and more subtle than that of tides or river floods, recording the rise and fall of the water table over months and years. We put our ears to them, as to a seashell, to hear the periodic rhythm of drought and deluge, the beat of seasonal change.

O N THE WAY HOME FROM HYANNIS the other evening, I stopped at the landing at Walkers Pond. It was a calm, warm summer's night; a gibbous moon hauled itself limply up into the eastern sky and shook itself like orange jello in the water below. It was a perfect pond, this, tonight, without a light or a voice to mar its shores of low black hills. I do not think there is another pond of its size left on the Cape that remains so unspoiled. I may never see it so perfect again.

Off to my right I could hear the hot roar of the Mid-Cape, less than a mile away, louder than the surf and seemingly more persistent. Yet it did not spoil my enjoyment of the pond that night. I knew it was really no contest which would endure longer, the pond or the highway. Against the majesty of the elements man is always a pitiable piece of chaff, blown away by the universal winds. In our bones we know it, and that knowledge has always been the source of our tragedy and our dignity.

No, the earth really has nothing to fear from man. The contest was created unequal. It is man that man diminishes by his recklessness and waste, simplifying himself as he tries to simplify nature and make it conform to his abstract desires, making it slick and facile, making it more difficult for him to belong to that which spawned and nourishes him.

T HE TOWN IS A DELIGHT to drive through these days, the snow firm and crunchy and wind-driven, impervious even to salt and plows, the streets full of long blue shadows, metallic coppery sundowns, the old houses standing firm and white, windows softly lit at dusk, reaffirming their old, close relationships.

Even if we are no longer a community in the old sense—sharing mutual needs and interdependencies tied to the local landscape—the houses, in their long-devised juxtapositions, ask neighborliness of us, preserve a template of the community that once was, a visible reminder of what we have lost to measure against the dubious gains of our more mobile, modular lives.

B Y THE SIDE OF THE WOOD ROADS, I frequently come on old bottle dumps, testaments to the casual disposal methods practiced by the former inhabitants, and sometimes mute evidence of the tenor of their lives here. In this land of geologic youth, the artifacts in these dumps strike me with the force of fossils, and must serve as such since the Cape can claim no real ones. There are heaps of broken crockery and plates, rusted pots and coal scuttles, pieces of broken farm implements, and lots of square, green-tinted bottles. These last are usually either medicine bottles—queer old panaceas and tonics of the age, whose curious names are spelled out in raised glass letters: "Mrs. Harvey's Cherry Elixir," "Beef, Wine & Iron"—or else broken whiskey flasks. Life wears out, these dumps seem to say, and people with them.

Just west of our house, below the rim of Berry's Hole, is a fairly large dump of this sort, containing parts of old stoves and water heaters as well as lesser debris, all discarded from an old house that once stood a few yards back from the edge. One day in early summer I was poking around this old dump when I became aware of small lavender petals falling to the ground all about me. When I scanned the woods to see what shrub or bush they might have come from, I noticed that the oak trunks were wound and cabled tightly with long, thick vines, some over two inches in diameter. The vines wound their way up into the forest canopy some twenty-five feet overhead, where, like exotic orchids blooming in some tropical forest, they burst out in masses of large, purple, pealike flowers that hung down in drooping clusters. It was the first time I had ever seen wisteria in the woods, and it was strange to think of these fragrant adornments of old Cape homesteads grown to monstrous wild form here in the dark shade of the oaks.

The inhabitants of the vanished house from which these vines had escaped were casual by repute. The rumor of an old murder lingered about the site, and the house itself had been dismantled over a decade ago. Now only a large old apple tree, the dump, and the escaped wisteria vines remain—a legacy of trash and blossoms.

Old bottles

Winter sunset

A T SUNSET I WALKED DOWN Red Top Road to the singing field to listen for woodcocks. Small things—quail, squirrels, voles—clicked and whistled and rustled and snapped away through the underbrush and last year's dead, dry, leprous leaves—stark, scraggly woods that not even the most partial of affections can call lush.

Stopping at Nate Black's old barber shop—the "Black Hills Emporium"— I rested against its weathered, shingled wall, looking across the road at the scarred field in front of the tumbledown old building with its black, vacant gable window. This whole place will soon be swept away, as the woodcocks have already apparently been evicted, by abstractions—because men may own land and turn it into a profit, because old roads do not meet the demands of modern engineering specifications, because magic—unless it is human illusion—has little, if any, recognized value in our society.

And this old field has been a place of magic, a fortuitous collection of natural ingredients—majestic, crumbling locusts, bats flitting in and out of sashless windows, box turtles crawling in the lush deep grass, deer gathered in tableaux at dusk, woodcocks arching and spinning up into the velvet, light-rimmed evening, crippled hawks weaving along the sand in the road—a rich gathering of life drawn to the long-gone center of human enterprise that once existed here, drawn as though to a magnet, as though life present can sense life past and finds more than ample browse and courting grounds in such a place as this, or at least, in finding these things, pays the past unconscious tribute.

LOCAL COLOR

Cranberry bog

THERE IS, IN OUR TOWN, a cranberry bog that I pass at least once every week. The owner is a man with an old Cape name and is, as far as I can tell, the only one who works the bog. At least he is the only one I have ever seen out on it. His tools are a hoe, a shovel, a wooden wheelbarrow, a turf axe, and that most useful of all native garden implements—the quahog rake. I have never met him, but I have observed him and his bog from the roadside off and on for nearly twenty years now.

The man is old, though I don't know how old, for he does not appear to have aged since I first noticed him. He has a weathered-clean appearance. Lean and tall, in faded blue jacket and cap, he has not become bent or shrunken with age, only more spare. Like a slip of scallop shell pared and polished by the wind and salt of the beach, he has been refined, not diminished, by the years.

His movements are sturdy and assured, as though his whole life has been unhurried and steady-paced. Watching him from the road, I seem to see him through a time warp, as though he were in some life-like historical diorama labeled "A Cape Cod Cranberry Grower." And he in turn seems to live and work in a world of his own, oblivious both to me and to the changing parade of vehicles and events that have rolled and roared on the highway and his bog over the years.

In late spring, after the danger of frost is past and the bog has been drained, he appears on the edges clearing scum and debris out of the ditches and off the plants and carefully trundling wheelbarrows full of sand out on planks to spread among the vines. Along the border of the bog are several white wooden beehives which he tends, hives which in June make his bog alive and seething with thousands of local insect workers pollinating among the small, white, nodding cranberry blossoms.

Throughout the summer he weeds and cultivates regularly with hoe and hook, nudging the bog to fruition, while about his head dip tree swallows which nest in the wooden houses he has placed on poles across the center of the bog. Day after summer day they patrol the vines, controlling many of the insect pests that molest the cranberry plants, while the young green fruit begins to darken to red, like holly berries, among the low leaves.

In September he piles up old wooden packing boxes in neat stacks along the bog's sides—many of them sporting labels from other, now-defunct local bogs. They remind me of the lobster pots piled along our saltier shores. During the harvesting, even he has replaced the slow, laborious handpicking by cranberry scoops with a more efficient mechanical harvester. But it is still a one-man job, and, unlike most commercial bogs, he still uses the "dry-picking" method, which allows his crop to be stored and sold fresh and unprocessed. By the middle of October a small hand-painted sign is tacked onto a tree by his entrance drive that reads "Fresh Cranberries."

After the harvest, as the persistent leaves begin to turn their winter, wine-dark color, I see him again out on the bog, pruning the vines by hand. Fresh piles of sand appear along the banks and again he wheels out sandloads to be spread, a shovelful at a time. With the last of the cranberry boxes gone, the last swallows flown, and the beehives wrapped for the winter, the bog is flooded again to protect the vines from frost. In the early dark of late December afternoons, I pass the bog and my eyes are caught by the string of colored lights wound around the pole of the empty birdhouses. And again, during January cold snaps when the bog is solidly frozen, I see him again out on the bog with yet another barrowful of sand, spreading it onto the ice to sift down among the roots at the next thaw.

I may, of course, read too much into this man and his bog. It is easy to do when you look from a distance and don't know all the facts. I sometimes think I have deliberately kept from making his acquaintance for fear of having my image of him spoiled by specifics. But even as suspicions rise, there is something in the cranberry man's simple movements that stays them: a deliberateness of action, a measured pace that suggests an inner peace, an affinity for his surroundings as though they were old and comfortable clothing. He exudes an unself-conscious sense of place, of possession by long and loving acquaintance, and his regular appearance on the bog at different seasons makes him a fixture in the local landscape, one of those human figures we cling to more and more as our own lives become more shifting, profitable, and abstract.

I ONCE READ THAT fresh cranberries are sorted for quality by being rolled along inclined wooden chutes, where they are given several chances to bounce over a series of baffles and obstacles. If they bounce high enough, they are considered sufficiently fresh and are packed away. The rest go into processed products. It seemed a fair and sporting process, one designed to let the berry show its stuff in equal competition. But who, I wonder, will help the grower himself leap or bounce over the baffling obstacles of his own life? Who will watch over him, through sleepless nights in pickup trucks beside his bogs, through the long frost-nights of his soul, flood him with protective waters when the wind might whip him to death, rent hives of bees to pollinate his life in its blossom-time, and nurture his low creeping

Harvesting cranberries

Wychmere Harbor, Harwichport

life to a red, ripe resilience so that he, too, may bounce high enough to break against the palate of a god? The cranberry, one thinks, is quite capable of returning the favor.

W̲E WERE HAVING A BEER in the Yard Arm after work one day when one of the carpenters told the story of Tim Donaldson, an entrepreneur from Harwich, who was charged several years ago with piracy. It seems he lifted an engine off a stranded dragger on the back side of P-Town. They had to let him go, though, for the mandatory penalty for piracy in Massachusetts is hanging on the Boston Common.

I̲ CAME AT LAST TO THE BLUFF above the beach, and there, at the very edge, stood Peggy Gibbs' old beach shack, its red paint faded, its windows unboarded and staring vacantly out at the Bay.

Once at a cocktail party Peggy, then in her eighties, told me of finding a note in the shack one morning from an anonymous couple, thanking her for "the most wonderful night of our life."

"Occasionally I think I should probably put a lock on it," she said, with a slightly apologetic tone, "but I haven't got the heart."

Even now the walls were scrawled with other simple testimonials to various trysts and passions over several decades, the last only a few weeks before. Inside the shack I found the sheet of plywood that had been used to board up the windows, with the words "DONT WREK THIS HOUSE" scrawled on it. Indeed, it seemed to me that this structure should be preserved and displayed, along with the town hall, the gristmill, and old sea captains' houses, as one of the more significant structures in our town's history.

THE OTHER DAY, walking up the hill on Stony Brook Road, I met Mrs. Scott, dressed in her habitual blue bathrobe, coming out to get the Sunday paper. She is getting quite lame and bent over now, walking slowly and painfully with a cane. She can no longer walk her dog Chinny out with her for fear that the dog would pull her to the ground and she wouldn't be able to get up.

She told me about a horse they had when she was a girl, a gray mare that would occasionally run away down over to the Black House, or over to Uncle Joe Ellis's place on Red Top Road. She would be sent to retrieve it since she was the only one the horse would come to—"No *man* could get that mare!" She wasn't supposed to ride the horse but she would get on it bareback and ride it at full gallop down Red Top Road until she came to the cross road, now my driveway, that connects with their house, get off, and walk it sedately to their barn.

Her family had a square root cellar in her tiny house, which was moved to its present site from East Dennis after the Civil War. It used to be packed with potatoes, turnips, onions, cabbage, etc.—and all the canned goods her mother used to put up. She was always the one sent to get the turnips since you had to climb over the potatoes to get to them.

She told me how, when she sold an abutting parcel of land about ten years ago, the money was delivered to a lawyer who was slow in getting it to her. She tried repeatedly to reach him at the office but could never get through, so she called him at home at 6:00 one morning, and each succeeding day one hour earlier until he paid her. "Folks think widows are easy marks. Well, some are."

A census taker came to her house recently and asked her how many rooms she had.

"Six," she answered.

The census taker stepped back and eyed the small half–Cape. "No you don't," he said.

"Oh—what happened?"

WEDNESDAY WAS WINDMILL MOVING DAY, and most of the town turned out to see it. Mrs. Nickerson's two hundred-year-old mill was moved some five miles down Main Street from behind her house in East Brewster to its new home in the field next to the Drummer Boy Museum in West Brewster.

School was let out for the occasion, and Brewster Elementary School students wrote poems and drew pictures in its honor. The utility company men who

Old saltbox, Brewster

Brewster windmill by moonlight

perched on the truncated top (the cap had been sent on separately the day before) wore self-conscious smiles, looking more like children along for the ride than serious workers. The move took two days and the windmill spent the night off Lower Road in Billy Dugan's cow field.

It was elating to see the rickety old structure burgeoning its way up Main Street like some grand old dowager—ancient, unwieldy, and dignified, so sunk in the proportions of her past that she could make no compromise of speed or efficiency with this modern society, demanding that the branches of the upstart century-old elms be pruned back, and that the even newer electric wires be raised like ceremonial arches for her passage. I loved it for its air of unbudgeable presumption of allowances due.

Dana Eldredge told me a story about Warren Baker, who was a lieutenant at the Old Harbor Lifesaving Station on North Beach during the 1920s. One time the station commander, a very strict and particular man, went away for a few days leaving Baker in charge. All went well until the day before the commander was due to return, when, somehow, the roof of the boathouse caught on fire (one of the men smoking, it was suspected, had flicked a cigarette onto the old, salt-dried wood shingles). The fire was put out quickly, without any real damage, but it left a large charred hole in the roof. Baker was beside himself. What would the commander say? They repaired the hole, using some old shingles they had stored, but had to use new planking underneath. If only the commander didn't go in the boathouse, things might be all right.

The commander returned the next day, and, with Baker, made an inspection of the station. Everything appeared to his satisfaction until they got to the boathouse. Baker stalled, but was unable to fabricate any substantial excuse for not going in, so he reluctantly and resignedly followed his chief inside. The old man's keen eyes swept around the building's interior, over the boats, the breeches buoys, and other lifesaving equipment with tacit approval. Then they rose upward to where the raw boards stretched out accusingly across the rafters.

"*Mister Baker!*" exclaimed the commander. "What is that?"

"Well, sir," the hapless lieutenant replied, "it looks to me like the roof of the boathouse."

The commander looked at him, paused and grunted—"So it does, Baker—so it does." He left the boathouse, Baker followed, and not another word was ever said about it.

Chatham band concert

Heading out for a sail

Pumping out rental boats

Repainting the West Parish Church, Barnstable

THEY ARE BUILDING A HOUSE these days on the far side of the kettle hole. Though the site is hidden by the trees, I can hear the familiar sounds of building: the rhythmic hammering and nailing of joists to sills, decks to joists, studs to shoes and plates, shoes to decks; the whining of Skilsaws cutting jackstuds and headers, crowsfeet in the rafters, bridging laths; the dropping and stacking of the plywood sheets, the hollow, staccato sound of the deck being nailed off; the playing of a radio, men shouting back and forth to one another in the open air with the harsh, sharp, direct tones of cooperation.

Catching me unawares, through the corridors of memory, they strike me as good sounds—whatever I might have wanted for that piece of land. The sounds of men building together in the sun: their noises come to me filtered through the thick summer foliage of the oaks, mixed with the soughing of the soft summer breezes through the treetops that wash refreshingly over this land almost every afternoon, and the songs of chickadees and bluejays as they hunt and peck among the branches and the twigs, hunting insects and the eggs of insects.

We sometimes forget, in this land under siege, that there is nothing *inherently* wrong in building a house—or in leaping off a dune for joy, or picking a bunch of sea lavender, or hooking a striped bass. We, too, are part of the earth's enterprise and passion and are meant to use her resources and enjoy her pleasures, and in turn to be used and enjoyed by her.

THE STORY GOES THIS WAY: Back in the 1920s a tourist was driving to the Eastham Life Saving Station when he passed Doane Rock, then called Enos Rock, the largest known boulder on Cape Cod. In front of the rock was an old Cape Codder, sitting on a fence. The tourist walked up to the man and said, "Mighty big rock."

"A-yeh," said the Cape Codder.

"How did it get here?" asked the tourist.

"Glacia' brought it," said the Cape Codder.

"The glacier brought it, eh? Well, well." The tourist paused. "And what happened to the glacier?"

"Went back f' maw rocks."

Glacial erratic, Brewster shore

Provincetown and Beach Point from the dunes

LYING ON THE BEACH AT LONG POINT, my legs stretched out toward the town that sat in unmistakable outline across the Harbor, I had, as it were, Province-town at my feet. This is surely the best vantage point from which to view it, nestled, in Joseph Berger's sly image, "like a piece of silver that has just crossed the palm of Cape Cod."

It is true that Provincetown is generally considered the most commercial of any Cape town, even advertising that fact in the name of its main street. But the gaudy human carnival that swamps its streets each summer is essentially a veneer, and at most dominates a small stretch of the town. More than any other Cape Cod town, I think, Provincetown has managed to remain a community, in the tradi-tional sense of that word—an identity unto itself. It is still primarily a collection of distinct neighborhoods, full, even in summer, of their local residents, tending gar-dens, paintings chairs, walking dogs, riding bicycles. It strikes me, in fact, as a kind of poem, not in any sentimental sense, but rather as fitting Robert Frost's hard-nosed description of himself as "a unity of bursting opposites." It contains a greater—and more notorious—ethnic and social diversity than any town over the Canal (not the least part of which is its high-level dosage of seasonal tourism and money), yet its diverse parts manage somehow not only to coexist, but to form a recognizable and vital identity.

Much of its visual appeal—that random compactness which is one of the few genuine examples left of the "Rural Seaside Charm" marketed like saltwater taffy by the Cape Cod Chamber of Commerce—depends, of course, on a certain consis-tency of architecture over time, marred only at its edges by ill-conceived high-rises and condos. But it also depends, as much or more, on the broad blue apron of the harbor that sets it off in front, and on the "palm" in which the silver coin of the town lies: the unspoiled setting of ponds, forest, and dunes of the National Seashore that backs up and surrounds the town in concentric, protecting layers.

The Provincelands, what the old Provincetowners always called "the outback," has defined and shaped the character of the town as much as anything else. Iron-ically, its public ownership—or public confiscation, depending on your point of view—has long been and continues to be a bone of contention. The people of Provincetown have always used the outback for their own purposes—cutting wood, pasturing cows, drying fish and fishnets—though it has been under public ownership—first colonial, then state, and now federal—since before the town was founded. Local inhabitants have always bristled at what they consider unfair and unnecessary restrictions. It is a question of suitable use that has been going on now for almost three hundred years, and it is not likely to be resolved soon.

Wood End Light, Provincetown

Blessing of the fleet, Provincetown

Long Point, Provincetown

But however enforced its preservation, it is Provincetown's unspoiled surroundings that also make it the last Cape example of the traditional New England village; that is, a tight cluster of houses surrounded by a preponderance of open space. It is the nature of that open space—the freely moving dunes, and the bright blue blade of the inner harbor, turning the eyes of the inhabitants around, curving us back to look at the rest of the Cape spilling down the inner shoreline of the Lower Cape, up the Sandwich Moraine, across the Canal, and finally around to the floating hills of Manomet across the Bay—that gives Provincetown its special position, its unique environs and perspective. Here we come to the end of things, standing at its tip and staring back to where we have come from, discovering that place anew, a "presence among us," as Archibald MacLeish said of the earth as seen by the first moon astronauts.

WATERY PLACES

S.S. Longstreet, *1990*

THE S.S. *LONGSTREET*: 1964. The target ship, we called it. The big ship, the target ship, the Liberty Ship. Before we knew its prosaic history, we imagined it a battleship hauled back from whatever unheralded glories it had known in World War II, not heroically sunk or even decently scrapped but ignominiously sat, plunked down in the Bay two miles off the Eastham flats, its belly resting on the sandy bottom twenty feet under at high tide.

For nearly two decades the fighters out of Otis Air Force Base had used it for target practice, pummeling it with target bombs and dummy rockets, not destroying it but, it seemed, mocking its enforced indestructibility with thousands of small gnat-holes ripped through its huge sides by the dull collision of dead metal on dead metal. Slowly, imperceptibly, its vast hulk rusted, rotted, fell in insignificant bits into the shallow water. There seemed something pathetic in its fate, that this piece of noble history should die, not in proud defiance of its attackers, but like some ancient show animal being slowly taunted to death.

For it was as a show you saw it then, from the shores of Eastham, Wellfleet, Orleans, and Brewster. It was imposing seen from the beach in the daytime, for at that distance it still retained its gun-gray appearance, the thickness of the atmosphere hiding the rust, looking sleek, indomitable, afloat. But it was best at night. Standing with the summer crowds on the docks at Rock Harbor or along the strands of Skaket, you watched the single, ominous red lights of the planes as they appeared, one by one, heading out across the Bay to the east, then circling slowly and steadily back across the dark water. Suddenly a huge cone of yellow light, emanating directly from before the red light, was thrown out across the black void, moving quickly, searching almost frantically, randomly, until the cone caught and instantly held its object: the vast, now-silvered hulk of the ship, half-lit and half-silhouetted in the glare, moon-like; or like some aboriginal sea beast finally tracked down in its watery lair by the furies of progress and marked for extinction.

The plane tilted down in a slow dive, the cone of light went suddenly out, and after two or three seconds of pure darkness (except for the small fierce moving red point of light) two to five bright soundless flashes burst well above the ship, while the spent shells fell uselessly and mockingly toward it, and you waited on shore again in darkness, silently and collectively counting the seconds somewhere between seven and eight until at last the deferred sound, burgeoning over the empty waters, fell in consummation on waiting ears: *Ka-thump. Ka-thump. Ka-thump. Ka-thump. Ka-thump.*

When it was over the crowds would casually depart, satisfied. It was often better than the drive-ins, and free to boot. It was all too naked to be a mystery, and yet among the residents it had come to assume the identity and the permanence of a monument, or at least that of a part of the local scheme of things, like the tide or the weather, with the latter's irregularity. Inland the target practice could be heard, day or night, clear to the ocean side, and people would stop momentarily, or turn in their sleep, and someone would say, or if alone, think, *It's the bombing*.

And on Skaket beach, where it could be seen clearly on sunny days, bright-colored bathers would saunter down to the water's edge and point their children to where the ship lay on the horizon in deceptively shallow water (so that it looked as if you could walk out and touch it) and tell uninformed myths about a history it never had and a future they could not imagine. It lay like a rainbow on the water, or a gray ghost—not so much a reminder as, by lying so heavily in the past, a duller to the memory of that man-spawned plague of war, lying only two miles and yet forever off the shores of this sun-drenched and inviolable American playground.

FLOUNDER FISHING, as anyone who has tried it knows, is meat fishing, not sport. There is no fish that is less of a challenge to lure to your hook, or that will give you less of a fight once you do.

On the other hand, what this fish lacks in fight it more than makes up for in amiability. I am talking now of the winter flounder, *Pseudopleuronectes americanus*, also known as the blackback or lemon sole. Just when many of the summer game fish are beginning to leave our shoal waters, the winter flounder arrives, almost, it seems, so that we will not feel deserted. Widespread and at home in shallow waters from Newfoundland to Georgia, the winter flounder requires little expense or effort to catch, and is so easy to land that a small child can do it—and often does so better than his or her adult companion. Being a bottom scavenger, the flounder will take almost any bait—sea worms, nightcrawlers, clam feet and necks, fish scraps, leftover chicken—and once it does it will obligingly lie there quietly so that a colleague may swim up and take the other hook. (Flounder are normally taken on double-hook devices known as spreaders.) They lack the numerous sharp spines found on many other game fish, enabling you to disengage the hook without fear of impaling your hand. They also rarely swallow bait, so that three or four fish can be landed without rebaiting. Because of their flat shape they also stack neatly and efficiently in the bottom of your bucket or fishbox.

Flounder fishing

Nauset Marsh, Eastham

Once brought home, flounder are, if anything, even more obliging. They do not need to be cleaned, but are easily filleted. They need only to be scaled or skinned on the top side. ("Top side" is a reference to the flounder's strange morphology. The adult fish is vertically flattened and swims along the bottom on its side, with both eyes on one side of its head.) And smaller fish, the ones that suddenly metamorphose into keepers at the end of an unproductive day on the water, seem to be purposely shaped for pan broiling. They are, in fact, the Shmoos of the marine world.

On the last afternoon of October, during a sweet stretch of balmy weather, a friend and I set off in his Boston Whaler with a couple of dozen nightcrawlers to spend a few hours flounder fishing on the calm and clear waters of Nauset Harbor. Anchoring off a sandy point, we each threw in two sets of baited hooks and waited for signs of gratitude from below. When fish are biting well there is usually not much time for anything but hauling in line, unhooking fish, and resetting. But the run of the tide was beginning to slow and the flounder with it, so that we had time to jiggle our tarred lines between thumb and fingers before pulling them up. (Though for some reason I have never hooked a flounder by playing it—it has either been there or it hasn't. I suspect jigging lines is just something flounder fishermen do to keep from feeling totally useless.)

Even without such a practical justification at the other end of your line, Nauset Harbor is a wonderful place to spend an Indian summer afternoon. A few lobster boats ride placidly at anchor. Hundreds of pots are heaped in mounds on the lower part of the beach. Partially submerged in the rising tide, they look like skeletal reefs, projecting menacingly out of the water. A cormorant fishes in the shallows, diving with little fillips and emerging again.

To the east the long white arm of Nauset Spit stretches northward longingly and empty. At its far end we can just make out some turbulence in the water, indicating the inlet channel entrance from the ocean, and beyond that the truncated arm of Coast Guard Beach.

New Island (which, though formed nearly twenty years ago when the southern end of Coast Guard Spit was cut off, will probably be called New Island until the flounder forage over its dunes) is much closer to us on the north, with a couple of more recently formed shoal islands trailing off behind. Beyond the islands, to the northwest, the bare grassy crown of Fort Hill lies shining in the October sun, prominent not only for its lack of trees but even more for its lack of houses. It is there that the National Seashore begins to take in the mainland as well as the beaches. "The nick of time" applies more vividly to the Fort Hill area than most, for when it was included in the National Seashore takings in the early 1960s, the hillside meadows had already been subdivided and marked with lot stakes and bulldozer tracks.

I seem to see the encircling scene more clearly than I do in summer, partly because the low sun lends contrast and shading to each feature, so that shapes resonate rather than blend. I realize, with something of a start, that relative to the winter solstice this afternoon is the equivalent of late February. How the tides of the season lag here, casting lengthening shades of reluctance and regret over all endings and partings. It is a wide and flowing place, and flounder fishing, not requiring much concentration or effort, is a perfect activity during which to contemplate its history and pleasures.

It is a lovely and a peculiarly empty day, as we sit in our small boat jiggling our flounder rigs in the clear green waters. Not only the summer crowds are missing, but many other recent noises and sights as well. Gone are the screaming clouds of common and least terns that nested all summer on the sandy plains of Nauset Spit and on the grass-covered dunes of New Island. Gone, too, are most of the shorebirds of late summer and early fall; only a few black-bellied plovers, a lingering yellowlegs or two, and flocks of bright sanderlings forage on the disappearing flats and along the tidal wrack. The migrating swallows that cruise the spartina prairies and the wandering monarch butterflies that straggle down the beaches in late September have all flown.

On the other hand, the large flocks of eiders that regularly feed on the estuary's mussel beds have not yet arrived, nor has the herd of young harbor seals that spend the winter months fishing its waters and hauling out on the frigid beaches of New Island. It is a slack time of year, a time between seasons and currents of life, between the growth of more salt marsh behind the dunes and the attrition of the Outer Beach in the face of winter storms. Like the flounder that we *assume* are hooked, waiting to be pulled up and turned into fish dinners, the year seems to be lying quietly at the bottom, waiting for some sea change.

For thousands of years men and women have fished the waters of this estuary and still the fish are here. That seems to me an incredible fact, even after the simple explanations of biology. Perhaps it is the more remarkable because of the increasing number of once-rich estuaries that are no longer productive, or because of the always imminent threat of oil spills along these shores. Somehow the flounder, the winter flounder, coming into our cooling waters to feed and spawn through the

Great blue herons at dusk

Scorton Creek, Sandwich

dead months, seem a symbol of the renewable and undying, though not inexhaustible or indestructible, riches of a place like this.

My friend, of a more suspicious nature than myself, wonders whether the offshore dragger fleets have, over the past several decades, affected the number of flounder available to us here in this protected embayment. It is difficult to determine such things, although the total flounder catch for New England has decreased more than 30 percent over the past half century.

It is a typical question from him. He is instinctively much more aware of the loss of fish, birds, other wildlife, and open land than I am. In contrast, I have to fight against an almost constant sense of undeserved richness and unexpected beauty. We have similar sensibilities, but it is a matter of differing backgrounds. He grew up here, took the land's abundance as his natural birthright, and so, in this era of rampant, blind development and exploitation of this land and its waters, he has developed an ingrained sense of diminishing resources and expectations.

I was born in an urban setting, on the glass-littered banks of a dead river whose dark waters glistened with the rainbow hues of oil slicks. I grew up expecting no more, so that when I came here, like most washashores I found myself in the midst of unwonted plenty. Overwhelmed with the improvement of my surroundings, I did not, at first, sense the eroding forces at work.

Since then I have become only too aware of the vulnerable nature of this natural richness and the implacable forces at work to rape it for short-term profit and short-sighted benefits. Yet, even after all these years, I still have to make a conscious effort to overcome this initial sense of undeserved riches, must force myself to know and to feel how much I am missing, might have had, and will have taken from me—lest I become just another pathetic refugee from the city, grateful for whatever scraps the developers might leave us, taking a kind of morbid comfort in what we have not yet become, aspiring only to stretch out what is left over my own lifetime.

Even the flounder, carrying next year's generation in their bellies, have higher aims than that. That evening, when I fillet them under sink light on the cutting board, I find rich, yolk-colored roe or pale white milt along the ventral openings of almost every fish—a promise of continuity, like the leaves and flowers of next spring's trees, already formed inside the tight budscales on the stripped branches of November's woods.

LAST EVENING I WENT DOWN TO THE LANDING to see if any marsh grass for the garden had been blown ashore by the recent three-day blow. There was surprisingly little grass, but the sun, a raspberry balloon, hung on the horizon, fretted with slats of smoke-blue clouds, at the end of a long tongue of sand running out beside the creek. The front row of the parking lot was already full for the display, and several families were out wandering on the exposed bars and newly greened patches of fringe marsh. Dark cries of yellowlegs pierced the gathering dusk as once again, on this spring night, people were discovering their own capacity for fascination here.

At the end of the long tongue of sand, well over a hundred yards out, I made out the figures of three adults—two women and a man—and five children, all young girls. As I walked out toward them the man was bending over a shallow embayment of water, holding onto the tail of a large female horseshoe crab which, bent at right angles, looked like a large dark-brown hoe with a ridiculously small and thin handle. He was a young man in his late twenties or early thirties with a light beard and glasses, and was being bombarded with questions by the girls about the piggy-backed crabs plowing through the sand. He had that look of good-natured exasperation on his face that comes with having to play the role of The Adult Who Knows Things.

"I don't know—maybe the little one is sucking milk from its mother. . . . *Nurturing*, that's the word I wanted, *nurturing*."

"David would say they're having sex."

"Well, all right—I guess so." The two women chortled as he tried to herd everyone back to the parking lot. Another girl protested, "No—this is good for our culture."

Then another: "Maybe he's having sex with his mother-in-law."

"Mother-in-law! C'mon girls, give me a break! Even crabs have some morals! C'mon now."

But three of the older girls, in bright yellow and pastel pink jackets and sweaters ran back to the edge of the pool, their shoes thoroughly wet, but not quite willing to go into the water with the crabs.

"Let's stay and watch them marrying—let's watch the wedding!"

"Yeah—I now pronounce you man and wife. You may now kiss the bride. You may now kiss the bride!"

They stood, watching over the breeding arthropods, innocent of natural history, but reaching out to them in an instinctive desire for contact, shoveling sand

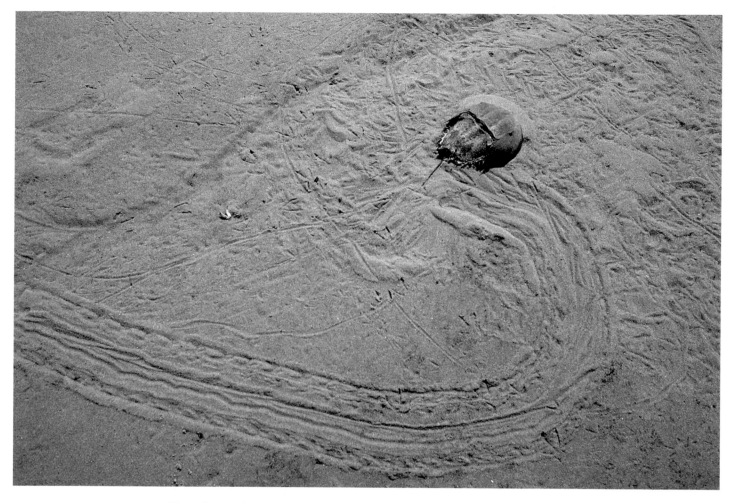

Horseshoe crab and track

Crabbing in the Mashpee River

over them with their hands, catching in the four hundred-million-year-old ritual they watched something of the universal currents and the fire that will touch them in a few years, here on these darkening sands.

And still they stayed, called by the receding, darkening figures of the adults. Finally two left, then the third, kneeling down to the crabs, murmured something over them, threw one more handful of sand, and ran after her companions.

I LIKE TO GO TO THE LOCAL CRAB CREEK late in the season, when there are fewer competitors. On an early September morning I dig out a package of chicken wings that have outlived their usefulness at the bottom of my freezer, or obtain a bucket of fish heads from a mackerel fishermen I know. From the small dock on the bank of the creek I tie the heads or wings to three lengths of flounder line, toss them into the murky waters above the bridge, and wait, waving cruelly to busloads of schoolchildren as they rumble by over the bridge.

It is an interesting experience, pulling in crabs this way rather than netting them by sight, for it is a kind of tug-of-war, but one that must be played with finesse rather than brute strength. The crab is, in a sense, caught by his own greed, or tenaciousness. Sometimes he will grab the bait and simply hold on, letting you pull him up out of the water, hanging on in mid-air, and even after you have transferred him into the net. More often, though, he will grab the bait with one claw and latch onto the bottom with the other, bracing himself, so that you must pull firmly, but not too abruptly, to dislodge him from his clawhold but not from the bait.

After a while I learned to distinguish which it was I dislodged, crab or bait, and if the latter, I let the bait remain on the bottom until he caught up to it and latched on again. It was a slow, careful ritual we practiced together, almost a court-ship. Several times a fish head left on the bottom too long would have its line snipped, by accident or on purpose. Usually I try to bring the crabs out of the murky depths close enough to the surface so that I could see them, then carefully sweep them from behind into the net. They seem to be able to see the net coming, even from the rear, so that frequently they slip off before I can net them, paddling off at a sideways slant with startling speed. When a crab is caught and dropped into the bucket with others, there is a brief aggressive flurry. Sometimes one cracks

Scratching for quahogs

Limpet shell uncovered by tide

the shell of another with its claws, but usually they retreat as far as possible from one another against the rim of the bucket, composing their claws in front of them like sleeping dogs.

It is a somewhat bloody, smelly business, this handlining for crabs—all chicken wings and bloody line and clacking crabs, while juggling snatches of coffee and donuts between rebaiting and line tending. But it is also a fine morning's contest, almost a character-building one, you could say: to see whose greed is more self-controlled, the crab's or mine. If he holds on too hard he loses; if I pull too hard, I lose. I have never been big game fishing, but it seems to require the same kind of inner discipline, knowing when to slacken off, when to pull in, and when to let go. In one respect there is even more *sport* to it, since there is, in this kind of crabbing, a choice on either end of the line.

O NE DAY RECENTLY I KNELT DOWN by the water's edge where not so much as a wavelet broke on the shore. The Bay, for the first time in months, was almost glassy smooth, with a soft southerly wind pushing the tide gently out. The past week, warm and calm, had not noticeably rearranged the beach. The carcass of a black-backed gull, spotted the previous Sunday, still lay undisturbed on the sands below the line of the last spring tide.

The birds had withdrawn. With binoculars I could make out clumps of brant, eiders, and scoters feeding a half-mile out. A single loon flew very fast and low over the water from west to east. Out beyond them I could make out more, unidentifiable birds in groups of ten to twenty spreading out to the limits of vision. On such rare days you realize that the Bay harbors a flotilla of thousands upon thousands of waterfowl just beyond shoresight and totally invisible when the water is the least bit rough or hazy.

My gaze returned to the sands at my feet where the rhythm of the tide slid in and out, noiselessly and without breaking, lacing the beach with delicate black tracings of sea grist. This dark grist, finest of all wrack, is made up of finely ground bits of seaweed, clamshells, pulverized crustacean skeletons, and other organic remains crushed beyond identification. Examining some of these thin, looping necklaces of sea dust, I saw that they were strung with innumerable empty shells of a tiny bivalve mollusc known as *Gemma gemma*, the gem clam. These are roughly

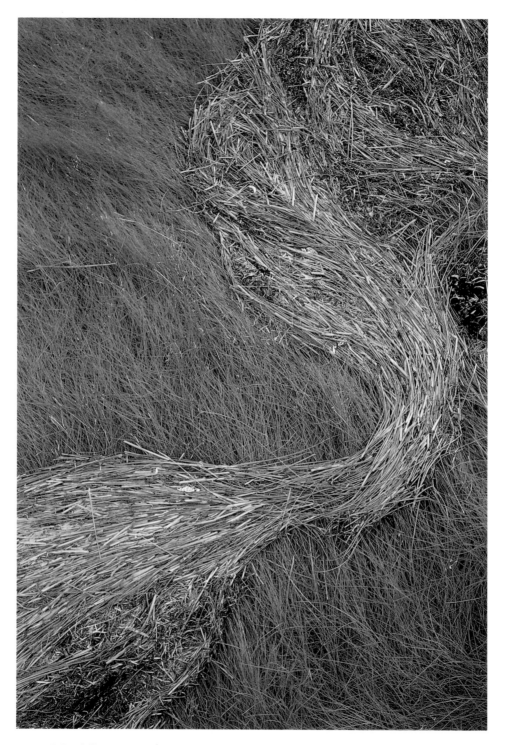

Wrack line on marsh

Patricia Marie *headed back to port*

triangular in shape and have a beautiful mother-of-pearl coating tinted with purple and finely crenelated inside edges. I picked one up—it was only an eighth of an inch across—and saw that it was pierced with the minute, perfectly beveled hole of a predatory oyster drill.

The fine crushed material, held in suspension at the very edge of the water, is on calm days like this deposited in dark, overlapping necklaces, creating intricate designs of three or four descending loops, until the next pulse of the tide sweeps in and erases all but the highest line. It was the ocean in a jeweler's mood, and the slight looping lines of wrack formed a nice contrast to the substantial mounds of marsh grass and seaweed heaped in a solid irregular wall several feet high that had been thrown onto the upper beach by the last storm.

It had a mesmerizing effect, like watching someone do close, careful work, with the constant slide and unraveling of the water, soundless and waveless, gently oscillating along the entire length of the beach. Out of such nothings does nature constantly create its marvelous, gratuitous expressions of beauty.

And it seemed to me, watching, that patterns in nature tend to mirror and echo larger and smaller elements of their own locale, particularly here on the beach. The shells of the flats imitate their surroundings, their overlapping ridges of growth repeating the mud ripples left by the tide. The running silver streams of water out over the sands on an ebbing tide reflect the streaming fronds of eelgrass over which they flow. A whelk shell repeats the curl of a breaking wave with the precise same geometric spiral. And so on and on.

And how many other Capes, I wondered, themselves necklaces of sand and geologic grist from ancient frozen seas, have been formed, thrown up, and then erased again by the flow and ebb of glacial tides?

FROM LONG POINT THE BLUE, WRINKLED, SHINING WATERS of the harbor lay peacefully spread out before me. A large blue-hulled dragger, whose name I could not quite make out, was moored a few hundred yards off the beach. The entire crew of seven or eight men were standing in a line on her port side, nearest me, shucking sea scallops and throwing the gurry over the rail, much to the delight of the raucous gulls swarming below.

The men stood at the rail in large yellow rubber overalls and short sleeves, with the intermittent sun beaming down on them and small flocks of winter eiders scudding by. They deftly slipped their knives into the yielding shells and flipped

Fisherman taking a break

Lobsterman, Orleans

Unloading bluefish

out the large "eyes," or adductor muscles. There was a rhythmic competency and camaraderie to their work, almost as if they were a band performing out there for their own pleasure.

But I knew, if only vicariously, the mortal seriousness of their work, whatever calm and even festive moments it may include. The ship's flag was lowered to half mast, in memory of the *Patricia Marie*, another scalloping vessel that had sunk with all four hands off the back side in Truro the previous week. Yet I could understand, in part, what has been termed the "irrational adherence" of New England fishermen to their ancient and (in the world's eyes) unprofitable profession and inefficient methods. They have outlasted this country's explorers, its hunters and pioneers, nearly all of its cowboys and most of its farmers. And if they survive oil rigs and factory ships, they will probably outlast our astronauts as well.

THE BAY WAS A MARVELOUS, SHATTERING SCENE of wind, sun, and water. The creek mouth and shore were glazed with cracked, sunken ice. The brown-stoned jetties looked like frosted coffee cake bars. The dunes to the east of the parking lot held the whipping beach grass and stiff, dark, flapping carcasses of last summer's sea rocket. A few white gulls stood out on the shorn marsh stubble, but most were soaring, flying for orientation, it seemed, and their white, eyebrow-shapes merged with the thin, moving whitecaps on the dark water that seemed to flake off from the dense, shattering line of white on the outer bar.

There were dozens of white peep scuttling like sowbugs along the grass stubble with the standing gulls, while a dozen or so black ducks poked about the edge of the peat ledges. Further out a white cluster of snow buntings wheeled across the creek and settled invisibly down on the shore ice on the other side. The low creek ran out in a series of stationary riffles, while a back eddy, pushed in by the wind, humped and plunged upstream on the far side, looking like more black ducks.

The protective ice-wall had already begun to form along the shore. All was stiff and hard, even the dark clouds that moved, hard-edged, against the cut-out clumps of pines to the west. It was like looking at a paper stage set, a three-dimensional scene made out of two-dimensional objects—a shadow box. I was not even tempted to get out. There was nothing to get out into. It was all forms and no substance. At the sky's zenith a large, salmon-colored, crab-shaped cloud hung over the entire Bay and crawled stiffly toward the declining sun.

Winter ice piled up on the shore

Off season

A CALM DAY, the Bay almost placid, the waters at Paine's Creek rimmed with a translucent collar of slush ice. Small rafts of eiders strewn calmly on the viscous, unbroken waters beyond, the tide running into the funneled mouth in full, cold, clear, green strength, chivvied by the faster wind-ripples flying over its surface. The tide was beating in, pulsing in over the sand shelf in rhythmic surges, throwing forward an arm of water, dampening and darkening the white sand, retreating momentarily, then beating in again, with no great advance each time, but unequivocally increasing its domain over each series of beats.

There were two or three other cars there, at dusk, as the dark silhouettes of gulls, like windblown leaves, sailed out over Freeman's Pond into the Bay. Not only are the gatherings at this landing superficially democratic—rusty pickups and Mercury Lynxes parked side by side—but their occupants all come for the most democratic of reasons: simply to see what is there. There may not be anything remarkable or even specific to see (this evening's sunset was dull, overcast, indeterminate), but it is as if the wideness of space itself, the openness, and the possibilities of that openness, draw us down to this spot. Often we get no farther than the front seats of our vehicles, but that is far enough to confront, to some degree, if only by contrast, the uncompromising originality of what we behold. It may not change our lives, but it will be an image we will never be able to lose or ignore completely.

D ROVE DOWN TO PAINE'S CREEK with coffee and a Danish this morning. The beach was white and clean with morning light, the marsh grass heavy and thick in the fullness of its growth, toppling over itself in windrows with its own accumulated mass, weighted like the heavy boughs of the apple tree behind our garden, its itchy blades its own fruit.

Beyond the lines of white bars and sky-blue shoal water, small white lobster boats, marked by their pug-like one-man cabins and laden with multicolored buoys and floats, plied the horizontal waters, leaving long white wakes behind as if their purpose out there were purely artistic, solely to extend the receding repetitive patterns of bar lines out to the horizon and so complete the pattern.

Low tide

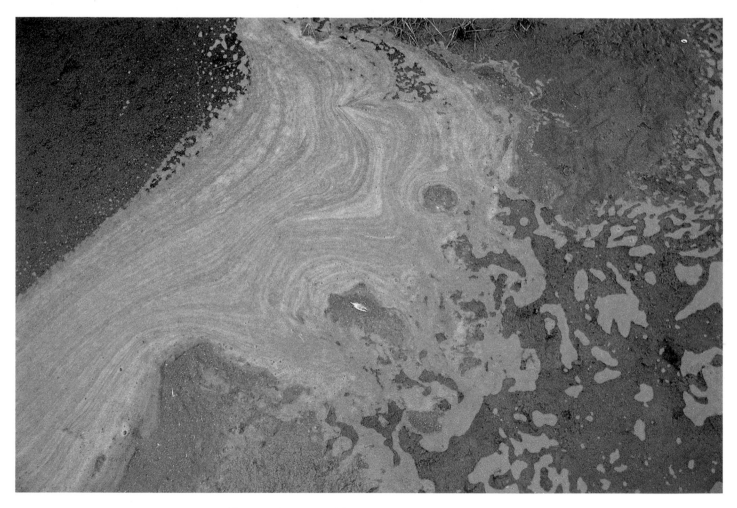

Patterns of foam on incoming tide

IT WAS A REMARKABLY PEACEFUL SCENE: a clouded sky to the east, filtering muted rays of sun down on a calm, almost glassy sea. The surf rolled in in long, measured curls, like the unfolding lip of a moon snail, and flocks of gulls spread themselves out on its silky surface as though on a pond. The slightly hazy forms of draggers plowed back and forth on the horizon. Who would guess that a week earlier, all was chaos? Or that, a day or two after the storm, the *Cap'n Bill* out of P-town with a crew of four was lost with all hands in one hundred and forty-five feet of water off Highland Light? Fishing is a strange mixture of the pastoral and sudden, wilderness violence.

WHILE WALKING ALONG THE INNER EDGE of a salt marsh the other day, I stopped to watch a finger of the incoming tide poking its way up one of the dry creek beds. It seemed like something alive, inching and probing forward, twisting and sliding among the interlaced ripple channels, veering off to one side and then the other, halting momentarily as though coiling and gathering strength, then striking out in a long, slow, sinuous glide for several feet.

Looking more closely, I saw that the lengthening, watery digit was populated. A hermit crab was scuttling about near its tip, a small marsh shrimp clambered over the sand grains just behind the crab, and behind the shrimp some sort of long, thin marine worm weaved its way along—all encased, like the organelles in an amoebic cell, in this moving, transparent finger of water.

The tide, advancing across the flats and up creek channels, often does this, creating numerous temporary marine aquariums, spreading out, for our approval and investigation, more organisms than we could assemble with a good deal of time and effort. Similarly, when it recedes, if often leaves its collections of shells, plants, and dead animals in the channels between the ripple marks, laid out neatly in parallel rows as though on museum shelves.

I played with the hermit crab a little, prodding him with my own finger to the very limit of the advancing tidal probe. He appeared frustrated that he could not run ahead any faster than his medium of escape was progressing, and tried to retreat, only to be blocked by a dark swatch of seaweed. I tossed him a few inches ahead of the moving channel and he stood there, rocking indecisively, as though he did not know his way back to the water and had to wait for it to catch up with him.

As I stood watching these creatures trapped within the thin, probing edge of the tide, the finger itself ceased to advance and stood there, marking tide, as it were. This was high tide, marked and underscored with a precision and definiteness impossible on the rhythmic, oscillating shores of the outer beach. It was as though the water itself pointed and said, "Here I stop—no further."

After no more than a minute, it began visibly to withdraw, leaving a narrow, winding, moist trail in its wake. I had that sense, as Emily Dickinson once did in the presence of the withdrawing tide, that we live, or survive, at the indulgence of some great global courtesy, a net of seemliness or manners thrown over the earth's blind and wrathful forces, a primitive lust of the sea for the land checked by some overriding decorum that we call the regularity of the tides.

IT IS A LITTLE AFTER FOUR NOW, and I am back at the fish pier, standing on the loading platform, waiting for my family. Less than a mile across Pleasant Bay, the cottage where I lived alone for a week sits clear and gray now under the first sun in three days. It seems so close, and yet years away, across the gleaming boat-plied waters. Below me crews in yellow rubber aprons fork the gutted flapping carcasses of codfish from their boat decks into a large metal hopper. When the hopper is full it is raised by a hydraulic winch and dumps its load, letting go a cascade of bloody disemboweled fish that goes sliding down a white ramp into the icy-breath'd hold of the packing plant. Though most of the fish will be shipped off to New York or Boston in huge refrigerated trucks, and though whole striped bass now sells for more than prime rib in the public fish market next door, we can still see the elemental processes of our survival in such places as this.

A young man on the dock calls to a friend who is just getting into a new green Toyota with a Connecticut license plate: "Those Canadian girls, they going to be back this summer?" The friend smiles, raises his thumb, and drives off. I smile too, content to be where I am, standing in this place of migrations and appetites, listening to the endless talk of fish, weather, and the chances of love.

Rock Harbor, Orleans

OTHER LIVES

Oystercatchers in flight, Stage Harbor Light, Chatham

I HUDDLE IN THE LEE OF A JETTY BOULDER and watch the gulls out at the edge of a receding tide. Beyond them, the Bay seethes and heaves whitecaps, a sea of wild horses. The wind, north and hard, peels the incoming waves off the surface like flesh being flayed. The gulls stand calm and unruffled before the fierce wind and the fury of dark water. They seem to exhibit a supreme nonchalance, an almost insolent indifference toward the violence of the shore, as though they were not hostages in the teeth of a forty-knot gale, but beachstrollers in a June breeze.

The nonchalance is, of course, a mask. Gulls are no more immune to the rigors of winter than are other birds. I find their stiff carcasses thrown up on the beach, nonchalant no more.

Yet these gulls, assembled in loose flocks on the lower beach, do not look as if such a fate awaits them. At least they do not seem to accept the earth's harsh terms with mere resignation. If anything, they seem to sport with it. Casually facing the gale, one occasionally opens its wings and, without beating them, lifts over the heads of his fellows and descends again. Then another does the same, then another. There they are, ballooning lazily and gracefully over one another, using the fierce energy that planes down land and water to play leapfrog, or leapgull, on the edge of destruction.

A hundred yards offshore, a flock of white-winged scoters beats westward into the wind, bodies stretched out, keeping low in the green troughs of the waves, wings beating rhythmically and in unison with intense purpose and great effort. "Keep close, keep together," their muffled calls seem to be saying, as though life were a matter of grim discipline. The hard lines of the day do not contradict them. Everything seems to press life down into lower and lower profiles.

Everything, that is, except the gulls sporting on the shore, or rocking carelessly aloft in the turbulence, for no good purpose except their own realization of flight. What is this playful leisure in the face of bare necessity? The result of perfect adaptation? Sheer stupidity? Or simply the lack of awareness (save for the mechanical reactions necessary for survival) of the stringency of the scene? Perhaps we ourselves have contributed to such behavior, offering them a cheap and easy food supply year round at our dumps, which may also have supplied them with a sense of security, a margin for living.

Cringing against my rock, I envy them their freedom, wherever it comes from. I see with what encumbrances of our vaunted technology I would have to weigh myself down before I could begin to stand out there with them. At various times all natural things display this sense of fitness; the gulls just show it off more extravagantly than most. I have watched brant feeding calmly in the shallows before the wall of a violent northeaster, and flocks of winter dunlins running up and down the outer beaches, skirting the grasping fingers of the breakers as though it were a game instead of a livelihood. Such freedom comes in part from knowing one's limitations perfectly.

In their apparent lack of concern, the gulls also seem to tell me that there is really nothing unusual in the scene, nothing to get excited about. I came out here to see grim, elemental struggle. Well, I found it, but they make me feel that my awe and elation are somewhat trumped up, only the emotions of a newcomer, a novice to wind and cold and inexorability.

They are right. Oh yes, the gulls seem to say, the beach might shift a little, scour out a jetty or two, undermine a sea wall, even break through a line of dunes—but that is all. We might make headlines out of it, and scurry about to protect our interests against these "vicious" storms, but the gulls know better. The quota of dead bodies, gulls and otherwise, will be about normal. Things will average out and the earth will hold. Yes, I can see that. Theirs is the perspective of a species, an outlook that values the processes that created and sustain them more than individual preservation. In such a view cataclysms are rare, even here on the shore. Mine is that of an individual, from a tribe that knows about this and future blows primarily through radio weather reports, newspaper photos and television newsbites, indoor barometers and anemometers—a kind of oblivion that is really more reckless than that of the gulls. Their insouciance deflates my easy sense of disaster. They seem at one with the old Cape Codders, also more in tune with the dimensions of weather, who spoke of such blows as a "breeze"—not out of false bravado but from a sense of perspective—and who did not build their houses on the sand, or if they did, did not expect them to last.

I WENT UP TO THE BEACH at the mill pond this morning and had the entire broad expanse to myself—not even a gull on the water. The truncated tupelo trees near the beach are turning red and green like a Christmas tree, with large dark-blue berries like ornaments. I almost stepped on a small, baby snapping turtle in the path about ten yards from the water. Only two inches long, it appeared fully formed, from its hooked beak to its ridged back and long, raspy tail. I picked it up by the shell edges and held it in front of my face. It stared back at me, this turtle homunculus—fiercely, unflinchingly, and impersonally—with the same directness

Dead herring gull

with which it would meet fate or a dragonfly larva. Its outlook on the world seemed one of implacable defiance which would grow only in size, not intensity or tone, and which did not, like that of men, change its outlook with the size of the problem or the foe. This little reptile exhibited as much unconscious principle (for what else can we call such steadfastness of outlook and comportment) as any person I have ever met: alert, yet calm as a rock, so unlike the caterpillar, say, munching blindly on, unable to dream of its fantastic, transformed future. I set it back in the water and left for lesser encounters.

I F EVER A CREATURE SEEMED TRAPPED BY EVOLUTION, it is the barnacle. Cemented for life to a rock or a piece of wood or glass by the back of its neck, entombed in a plated shell of its own making, a barnacle's horizons are not what you would call unlimited. Yet, it begins life as one of the freest of creatures, one of those untold billions of microscopic, floating planktonic larvae with which the sea is infused each spring. After several weeks of casual drifting and feeding, the baby barnacle descends to the floor of the ocean, where it deliberately examines its surroundings before choosing a suitable substrate on which to anchor itself forever. Once attached, the barnacle's way of life becomes extremely circumscribed and unadventurous, with seemingly little room for improvement or experiment. It works, period.

But the beach, newly salted with barnacles, reminds me not to judge a species' destiny by the individual's fate. There seems right now an unusual amount of young barnacle spat on the rocks, covering every square inch of open surface, which must have set within the last several weeks. Some, I see, have even settled on the backs of periwinkles, just as tiny baby periwinkles sometimes hide out in empty barnacle shells. Given that roughly the same amount of bare rock surface was similarly colonized last spring, little of last year's crop seems to have survived.

On the larger boulder of the jetties the barnacles provide a good gauge or water mark of mean high tide, for it is here that their numbers usually stop. Yet above the established white line of adults I see sprays of new spat—smaller, grayer, and still thin-plated—splashed up onto the rock two or three feet above their elders, thinning out at the very top, where only the last reckless pioneers of the new barnacle generation have established a precarious and temporary neck-hold, much like mountaineers symbolically reaching a pinnacle they cannot inhabit.

Sunlight under a dock

153

East Dennis from Sesuit Creek

These young spat, however, do not have the option of retreat. Each year some of the young try to colonize these upper reaches. During the summer, desiccation and a scarcity of food thin their ranks and inhibit growth. The following winter storms and ice scrape off the small empty shells and the remaining live ones, wiping the slate clean for next year's futile attempts.

One could see it as just another illustration of that prodigious waste inherent in all marine procreation. Yet who is to say the urge to transcend physical barriers resides in the human breast alone? Here in these doomed upward thrusts of these young barnacles into the unknown may be seen, quite literally, the species' margin for error—and extension.

I WALK NORTH TO THE END OF THE SANDSPIT, thinking to end the day with a swim in Hatches Creek. The tide is coming in, pushed by a strong, hot, westerly wind, so that the Bay rolls and lifts with summer whitecaps. A few bathers are scattered along the beach, but the wind and blowing sand are fast driving them off.

I strip off my clothes, wade into the tidal creek, swim hard for a hundred feet or so, then relax and give myself up to the landward movement of the tide. The water is quite warm, almost tepid. It must be nearly eighty degrees at the creek entrance. I am carried swiftly on the incoming tide, surrounded by seaweed and patches of furred algae, floating like a piece of flotsam myself, buoyed up by water so warm as to give the illusion of weightlessness.

Birds come to me. A flock of grackles flies by, heading out to the beach. A green heron, burnished dark in the sun, crosses the creek directly overhead with deep, arched wingbeats. A small flock of roseate terns chivies and circles above me, a strange fish. Some least terns join them, with their sharper, scissor-like calls. What perfect, simple designs the terns must see: sun, sandspit, weaving blue tidal creeks and waving green salt meadows—reassuring designs of life. The terns themselves seem molded to such elegance, spiraling down to spear marsh minnows.

I turn over on my stomach and see the dark, darting shapes of killifish, the short bright forms of silverside minnows, and, right below me, a small school of sand eels—thin, eel-like fish as long as my hand that glisten and undulate in the deep, green, clear waters. They blend remarkably in their element and even seem to align themselves with the wavering patterns of light refracted from the surface ripples that flicker along the creek's bottom. Talk about adaptive coloration—here are fish evolving into shimmers of light!

These sand eels form one of the principal food sources for our local terns. I have watched these graceful birds many times diving into creeks and offshore waters and coming up with coiling silver ropes in their mouths that flash in the sun. Their vision, in this respect, is much more refined than mine, as it not only has to pick these fish out beneath a sparkling, broken water surface, but also to correct for water refraction in their dives.

It is not surprising that these two organisms—tern and sand eel—locked in a mortal relationship for ages, have each become such sculpted, refined representatives of their respective mediums. Over the ages the sand eel's form has become less and less discernible in the water, the tern's eye keener, the eel more supple and elusive, the tern more adept and skillful in pursuit, and so on, until—what? Until the tern can catch light itself and the fish move in the grip of wind and sun. In elemental struggle this pair moves toward an almost disembodied perfection of fitness.

THIS EVENING, DOWN AT PAINE'S CREEK, I saw a silhouette of a shorebird against the new green of the marsh, and thought of it sympathetically, there along that grassy edge of land and sea, picking up nourishment where it could, solitary and unconcerned, intent, sure-footed in that slipshod world of the mud flats—a thin, rocking creation of this reedy shore, that suddenly kicks up its long legs behind and flies off low and straight, uttering a clear four-note whistle—the yellowlegs call—ahead of its flight.

OUT ON THE DRY, GRAVELLY SANDS the shorebirds of August group themselves in small tight flocks, sanderling with sanderling, plover with plover. They come in with the tide, pushed by a strong, hot, southwesterly wind that makes the waters of Cape Cod Bay heave and lift. Shorebirds are the Cape's midsummer fall spectacle. By August, when most of us are still looking forward to our summer vacations, the season has long been over for most of these long-distance migrants. Black-bellied and semi-palmated plovers, whimbrels and dowitchers, godwits, turnstones, knots, dunlins, sanderlings, and sandpipers—all are northern, largely Arc-

Yellowlegs fishing

157

Shorebirds waiting for the tide to fall

tic nesters that have only a few short weeks in which to court, mate, lay eggs, raise, and fledge their chicks. Most chicks are ready to fly three weeks after hatching, and the adults leave shortly after. Of the fourteen species of fall shorebird migrants that are listed as common or abundant on the Cape, thirteen arrive here in numbers in July. A few, such as the least sandpiper, show up in late June—heading south.

The black-bellies, largest of our plovers and one of the most abundant fall migrants, are in various stages of molt. Some still wear full, velvet breasts and face masks; others are mottled, with a tattered, mange-like appearance. From the sands in front of me a flock of ringnecks, or semi-palmated plovers burst out of nowhere, a sudden, spontaneous beach generation. A pair of lesser yellowlegs flies up from the group of sanderlings, white rumps flashing like flickers', uttering their urgent *chu-chu* calls. A short-billed dowitcher feeds quietly in the mud of a marsh pool, and beyond it a pectoral sandpiper.

Fall shorebirds, like fall warblers, are difficult to identify. Though they show a greater variety in size than any other bird group, there is a compelling underlying unity about them, a strong common denominator of shape, sound, color, and movement that is born of a shared life of high, wind-hewn journeys and northern tundra breeding grounds.

Yet though shorebird plumage, especially in autumn, shows very subtle variation, these differences are nonetheless remarkably fine-tuned to their habitats, even in migration. The piping plover (one of our few resident nesting shorebirds), with its pale-buff back, frequents the upper sandy beach, while its very close relative, the dark-backed semi-palmated plover, prefers the lower pebble beaches and mudflats.

To know them now is to master the earth's subtleties. They shift and blend on the sands like a set of Bach variations, subtle works of form and movement rather than of color and high romance.

WHEN I SAW THE WHALE, it was like seeing a ghost. There, some two miles off Race Point and about a half-mile ahead of the *Dolphin III* as she bore down, a large black glistening shape broke water. As it slowly arched across the surface, a small dorsal fin toward the rear identified it as a finback, second largest and most common of the remaining great Atlantic whales.

The finback continued to surface regularly every few minutes as we slowed speed and drew cautiously near. Finbacks, more wary than the popular humpbacks, normally steer clear of boats, but this one held its ground as we approached, and gradually it began to come into incredible focus. It spouted with a low rush of sound and speed each time it surfaced. The immense tail flukes are rarely seen except when it has refilled its lungs completely and does a "sounding dive," disappearing for twenty minutes or more. But the boat followed the trail of calm, circular swirls on the surface, each as large as a swimming pool, made by the tremendous thrust of the flukes under water.

Aside from the blue whale, the finback is the largest animal ever to live on the earth. This one was over fifty feet long and displaced about as many tons of water. Yet it moved with an unparalleled grace of motion. I have been told that even when whales are moving at a top speed of twenty knots or more, they exhibit this appearance of unhurried slow motion. Scientists explain it in terms of aerodynamic shape, "laminar flow" skin action that reduces surface friction, and other such cetacean physical adaptations; but the essence of it is far from unique in nature. Swallows, alewives, and deer all share with whales that same product of perfect adaptation to their chosen medium of life, a blending of form and function that humans have always responded to as natural beauty.

The whale continued to appear alternately on opposite sides of the boat, as close as fifty yards, and we realized with involuntary goosebumps that in between the whale's huge bulk was passing unseen directly beneath us. Then once, unexpectedly, it surfaced directly ahead, less than seventy five feet from the bow. Crossing slowly to starboard, it seemed deliberately to exhibit itself to us. First its immense dark head appeared, followed in slow succession by the blow hole, the long right side (colored lighter than the left), then the dark back arching up, followed by the dorsal fin. . . . On and on it came, like some great wheel of life, passing us endlessly like the long, curled sandspit of Long Point itself, and like that spit, shaped and sustained by the ocean.

I STOOD AT THE EDGE OF A FREEZING INLET, lines and colors edged and deepened in the dying light of day. Formations of geese flew, honking, overhead, directly into the sunset. What a different world's experience theirs must be! Up in the frozen air, winging in loose community, their dark eyes set and staring unlidded into the sun, glinting in the cold, red, reflected fire, a frozen blue and white waste below them. We cannot impose our sympathies and desires on them; in that world, they are beyond us, removed from any possible presumption of kinship or connection to our experience. They live in torrents of wind and channels of light that leave us wondering in futile admiration below.

Canada goose preening

Baby sea robin

Small snail on quahog shell, tide rising

A TRIO OF CROWS CONGREGATES REGULARLY now in the oak branches above the compost bin, though I have not yet seen them descend and eat. They do not seem like birds at all; even their feathers seem made of some slick fabric, stretched over their real bodies. They have neither the bewildered, amazed look of most passerines, taking in more than their little brains can think about, nor the hard, cold, impersonal stare of raptors, whose minds seem wholly lodged in their eyes, talons, and wings; but a gaze of reserved and slightly bemused curiosity, a warm-blooded mammal gaze, as though they really thought about what they saw, as though they had opinions about the world.

Their actions support this apparent visage. This morning, at breakfast, I looked out the window and saw a crow flying through the woods toward the house, landing on a branch for a few seconds, flicking out its broad, black, stiff tail in powerful, instantaneous thrusts, like a camera shutter, then flying on to another branch. It occurred to me that the crow had nothing to do with the trees, except to land in them. It sought no food there, chiseled no nest. It is a backdrop, a platform for it, as our local environments are for us.

The scene was one of overlapping hues and textures of gray: a thin veil of bluish-gray smoke drawn down from the chimney and across the yard by the mist; the maze of vertical and acute oak trunks and branches tinged with brown streaks; the far backdrop of oak crowns on the slope beyond the glacial bowl to the south, reddish-gray like exposed nerve clusters; and above them, the blank milky gray of the sky. And there, in the middle-foreground maze, having nothing to do with it all, sat the crow, black cynosure of the morning.

TODAY MY SON AND I WERE OUT IN THE GARDEN, poking seeds into the earth, when I thought I heard several peewees calling overhead—high, thin whistles. I looked up and saw, wheeling high, high up in the brilliant blue sky, a trio of broadwing hawks hovering up near the sun. They seemed an emblem of the season itself released from the winter earth, buoyed up on its own warmth and light. They banked and whistled and slid out of sight over the ridge of trees to the east. How thirsty my eyes have been for hawks! Their wheel is so different from that of the gulls' open soaring. The hawk is connected to the earth as he circles above it, his arcs describe it, his eyes survey it.

Crows in a cedar tree

Hanging in the wind

I WENT OUT TO THE BAY BLUFFS yesterday to watch the sea ducks in a rough northerly wind. Some mergansers were swimming close in to shore. Their long red bills and white wing patches appeared and disappeared with each rise and fall of the rough sea, like pupils in a crowd of winking eyes. Farther out a half dozen or so gannets skimmed and swerved over the sea, translating the surf's jagged chaos into the swift, smooth grace of their flight. And in the far distance, scattered lines of scoters and eiders crossed back and forth across the Bay like loom shuttles threading the woof of the waves.

But what struck me most that day was the sight of a merlin, a small falcon, poised some twenty feet above the dunes just behind the beach. It hung there, in a northwest wind of at least twenty knots, in perfect unchanging position for thirty to forty seconds at a time, giving only the slightest flick of one wing or the other every few seconds to maintain its place—neither rising, dropping, advancing, nor retreating an inch from where it had perched in mid-air. There were enough high, motionless clouds in the southeast sky behind it that, for the first time, I could determine how absolutely perfectly it maintained its position: its thin tail straight out behind, its dark arced wings hooding the rushing air. Except for the occasional wing-flick it could have been pasted there against the pale sky. Yet nothing bespoke dynamic motion, controlled kinetic force, the perfect engine of feather and wind so powerfully as that small, dark figure hovering over some unseen prey down among the bleached, wind-blasted beach grass. I might have been there for days watching it, while earth and sky and water all wheeled about it. It possessed what Frost called "master speed" against the universal currents, and made of itself the powerful pole-star of that mid-day scene.

LATE IN THE AFTERNOON I WENT CLAMMING off Robbins Hill Beach, walking a half-mile out on the flats where sand and channels made disappearing zigzags of green and yellow toward a lowering horizon. I found, at the edge of the receding tide, only lapping green water, and seaweed pieces, and little white caplets beating out to sea against a stiff, southeast wind. But a large gull came, first banking low against the beach so that his wing almost drew fine lines in the sand, as if he would be a sand artist. Then he came into the wind, but never quite landed, keeping his wings curved out, like great gray umbrellas, while his orange feet skipped along the shallows, walking, but weightless—a thing intent upon its own realization of flight.

Autopsying stranded pilot whales

Some toads have taken up residence in the crawl space, finding it, presumably, comfortably cool, dark, and damp. They seem strange, imprisoned bits of life. Their bodies are loose rubber bags palpitating at the throat and the back of the neck. They stay half-buried in the sand, inanimate and impersonal spectactors, watching the cool and the dark. Except for their quick, jewel-like eyes, that have seen everything forever, they seem like life attempting to return to immobility.

Several hundred feet ahead of me a fairly large object lay on the upper beach, which I took at first to be a log of some sort. But as I got closer it appeared to be furry—a seal, perhaps. When I came to it, though, it was a deer—a good-sized animal stretched out and half-buried in the sand. It lay on its side with its right hind leg extended gracefully behind, as though in the act of running. But its head was bent backward one hundred and eighty degrees and in its mouth was a sprig of rockweed. The eyes were intact, but the gulls had been at its torso (their drawn-crossbow tracks patterned the sand around it), exposing the ribcage, through which I saw a dark green mass of entrails. The genital area was eaten away beyond identification, and the exposed muscles of the flanks were striated a cold, marbled gray-blue and ivory. There were no other marks on it. It appeared to have been thrown up by the last tide and its limbs were not yet stiff. It may have been chased into the surf by dogs and drowned. Deer seem to flee into the ocean to escape predators the way whales seek the beach when injured or ill to avoid drowning, preferring a larger, more abstract danger to a smaller, more immediate one. Both remind us of the implacable terms of existence, what it means to choose the reality of the physical world in which to live, where there is no escape, only a choice of fates.

A Landscape in Motion

Beach buggy trail, Truro

OVER THE YEARS one of the foci of my wanderings about the Cape has been Nauset Spit, the southern half of the two-pronged barrier beach system enclosing Nauset Marsh and Nauset Harbor. I am drawn to it partly, I am sure, because it was on this beach, over half a lifetime ago, that I first encountered the mystery of the ocean and its peculiarly human relationship with this land. Since then I have returned here countless times. At all seasons it partakes of the richness of the marsh and the inlet it protects, and attracts at all seasons an uncommon share of life. During the summer months one of the largest least tern colonies in Massachusetts nests here and fills the plain with the noise and motion of these tiny shorebirds' goings and comings with an endless procession of fish for their young. Now, in winter, not only the terns, but the signs and fences that had marked and protected them were gone, all traces of this great annual avian adventure smoothed away, like a summer carnival that folds its tents and disappears down the road after Labor Day.

In winter visits I have scattered congregations of a thousand gulls from its sand flats and stalked visiting snowy owls. I have watched great reaping, diving clouds of common terns wheeling over the blue waters of the inlet in September, formations of wintering geese arriving out of the dark skies of November, and cast for the hidden running hordes of winter flounder on raw April days. And in July I have joined the summer crowds who walk or boat or ride out to the very tip of this spit's sandy point, gravitating as people will to any land's end, to stare and stare out endlessly over the dark rushing waters.

One New Year's Day I arrived at the beach a little before 6 A.M. It was cold, about fifteen degrees, clear and still dark. The lightest breezes flowed out of the northwest, due to turn northeast and bring in some snow by late afternoon. Offshore a high bank of smoky clouds delayed the coming of dawn, while three lighted ships moved slowly and smoothly north along the horizon.

The sea was calm and flat gray, a sheet of shimmering metal. The tide was low and rising with small breakers purling and curling in, spreading out from the middle in both directions like the final, quiet, repeated chords of Barber's *Adagio for Strings*. I took a last sip of coffee, pulled up my hood, and got out of the car.

Setting off north toward the inlet, I kept to the inner edge of the sandy, marshy valley that runs between the dune ridge and the bluffs of Nauset Heights. My bones were still cold from sleep, but steady movement soon warmed them up. The backdunes wore a winter-blasted look: shredded skeletonized cedars bent backward with heavy dark-green crests. Ragged, wiry, gray mops of poverty grass dotted the colorless sand between irregular brittle mats of lime-green reindeer lichen. The wind scythed through the wheat-colored beach grass, stirring dry stands of old cattail reeds and setting them to rattling like sabers. In the weak yellow light that now began to seep in from the east the only bright spots of color on the landscape were the shriveled Chinese-red rose hips, dangling like forgotten Christmas ornaments from the bare, rounded, spiked clumps of beach rose.

I circled round a small brackish pond whose northeast shore was frozen solidly and piled with rough ice by the wind. In the sand patches between broken clumps of toast-colored beach grass I found rabbit spoor and the tracks of other small mammals that must fight for existence year round in this place. Near the edge of the pond, among the locked reeds, was the body of a black duck, half-encased in ice.

Along the sand beach-buggy track I came upon the bodies of two murres—sleek, penguin-like birds whose lower white breasts were matted and stained with yellowish oil. These were victims of a relatively small oil slick that had appeared off Nauset the week before—the result of illegal but still routine bilge cleanouts by oil tankers, spills too small to be reported other than in the local papers, but whose cumulative effect on seabirds each year remains greater than that of all the major accidental oil spills that receive national headlines.

I continued north, past the dunes and out onto the flat, sandy plain beyond. Here I began to encounter more bodies of dead birds, partially or nearly completely covered with drifting sand. I kicked up the carcass of another murre and two horned grebes, all recently dead and showing evidence of oiling. There was a headless cormorant and a headless brant, two large Canada geese and numerous carcasses of gulls in their characteristic smashed or slapped down postures. Many of these had been worried at by dogs as well.

After a time I stopped kicking up and examining the dead forms. The distinction between human and natural death began to blur and lose significance in such a place. This wide, open, sandy, gravelly plain is surely one of the great natural stages of this or any other land, a broad, trembling lip of the earth in close and daily flux with the swirling waters around it. It is constantly changing in shape and visage, yet possesses a kind of submissive power and integrity born of its naked exposure. Here, in winter, among a graveyard of birds serving as their own half-hidden markers, this plain speaks of bare survival, without benefit of man's flattery, whose only mercy is the driving cover of the wind.

Condominiums massed behind dunes

In memory of
CAPT. HENRY SEARS,
who died
Feb. 22, 1839,
aged 63 years.

Also his son
HENRY SEARS, Jr
who was drowned
April 15, 1825,
aged 18 years.

Gravestone of a drowned seaman

O N MY WALKS ALONG THE SHORES AND SAND SPITS of this shifting peninsula I frequently encounter signs and tablets commemorating some past human enterprise. This is not surprising, given that the Cape has been explored, settled, and used by Western man for nearly four centuries. What is remarkable, and indicative of the special character of this place, is how many of these plaques and monuments are located at the extremes and edges of its boundaries, and the nature of the undertakings they commemorate.

Most historical plaques in places like Boston or Concord tend to commemorate famous battles, the founding of institutions, or the sites of vanished buildings—usually in locations that have been supplanted by more intense modern settlement. They tend to attest to the rootedness and continuity of life in a place.

The Cape, too, has its share of these. But the memorials I come upon most often during my walks tend to record, not permanence, but temporary outposts, points of departure or brief contact, and signs of extreme probing—like the stiff flags we have placed upon the moon or strongboxes with our signatures chained to the tops of mountain peaks.

Along the cobbly beaches that line the sheltered inner shores of Nauset Harbor, there is a large glacial erratic sitting in the intertidal zone. Affixed to its side is a brass plaque. What catches the eye first is a line of Gaelic at its botton: "Na laga din iad." Above it is the legend:

A FIGHTING CHANCE
JOHN RIDGEWAY AND CHAD BLYTH
ROWED ATLANTIC IN *ENGLISH ROSE III*
FROM ORLEANS TO KILRONIN ARAN
IRELAND. 4 JUNE 1966–3 SEPT 1966

At the National Seashore's Marconi Site in South Wellfleet, there is another plaque, a bust of Guglielmo Marconi, and a model reproduction of his original wireless transmitting station. All of this commemorates the spot from which man first leaped out across the Atlantic in insubstantial waves of polite and kingly conversation between President Theodore Roosevelt and Edward VII of Great Britain, though the actual radio station is long gone and several of the transmitting tower foundations have fallen into the sea.

There are even plaques for which there is no longer anything left to memorialize, or even anything left to attach them to. One such is the brass tablet that was affixed to the Fo'castle, Henry Beston's "Outermost House" on Eastham's Coast Guard beach in 1964, designating it as a National Literary Landmark. The ocean claimed the little house, in which Beston wrote his famous book of that title, during the Great Blizzard of 1978. The tablet was later found and now rests, like a gravestone without a grave, at the Wellfleet Bay Audubon Sanctuary.

Of course, the majority of Cape memorials should be placed where they obviously cannot be—at sea. Instead, generations of Cape Codders have had to content themselves with displaced memorials: "lost at sea," "went down with all hands on . . ." "drowned in the great gale of . . ." and similar legends inscribed in almost every one of the numerous little churchyards and burying grounds that dot this landscape.

All, all of these markers and memorials are testimony to the observation that the Cape's shorelines and tenuous extremities are not for permanent habitation, sheltered lives, or final answers, but rather for temporary structures only, expeditions of the feet and mind, unending voyages for the spirit.

I REMEMBER ONCE LOOKING THROUGH A COLLECTION of old photographs of Orleans taken around the turn of the century by a remarkable man, Henry K. Cummings. He was the proprietor of the H. K. Cummings Dry Goods Store in Orleans Center and, in his spare time, one of photography's self-taught "primitives."

From the roof of his old two-story wooden building Cummings shot panoramas of the barren, prairie-like landscape of the early 1900s, when nearly every resident, whatever his income or social position, had a saltwater view and probably wished he didn't. From the front steps of his store Cummings recorded the passing seasons in the center of town. From porches, along back roads, and on the local beaches he captured the faces and character of his friends and neighbors in formal pose, everyday work, and stilted play. He had an eye for the synoptic and the epitomal, so that his prints seem to capture the essence of his time and place, a talent that can only belong to one possessed by a sense of things passing.

I was struck in particular by two photographs taken at the very head of Town Cove, a seascape that in its treeless borders and faded contrasts looks like a lagoon at the edge of a desert. Both pictures were shot from almost precisely the same point, the first in 1887, the second in 1890. In the first, at the very edge of the water,

Le Count Hollow, Wellfleet

there is a row of the typical fishing shacks of the day: small, leaning, shingled buildings banged together from whatever materials lay to hand, with an eye to expedient utility rather than quaintness or substance, where scallopers and lobstermen and bullrakers shucked and culled their watery harvests.

In the second photograph this collection of working shanties is completely gone—not a trace remains. Though it was taken three years after the first picture, the background appears so identical and unchanged that the effect is as though the next tide had simply risen up and swept the beach clean. This fate, of course, frequently did and still does occur to structures on the more exposed ocean and Bay shores, but in this case it was the less predictable but no less inexorable tides of economic, social, and technological change that had done the work.

In his photography, between measuring out bolts of poplin or stocking fisherman's boots, H. K. Cummings created remarkable visual memorials, compressed plaques of glass and silver bromide, whose images attest to a truth which is still proclaimed no less clearly today to anyone who will walk these beaches and see where it is he walks: that we all live at the edges of time and space and at the implacable sufferance of the ageless interaction of those two forces, symbolized by the dancing shapes at the edge of sea and shore.

Like the terns and the warblers, like the harbor seals and the striped bass, like the great whales and the multitudinous alewives, we are all only transients here, or at most migratory residents. And so we had best set up our little oyster shacks and boathouses as expediently as possible, not worrying too much if the roof leaks a bit or the sashes stick, but culling and dragging what we can from the surrounding waters of our lives before the millennial tides come in and overwhelm us.

O NE DAY IN EARLY JUNE, having spent the morning in the woods, I walked a mile or two west and soon came to Cape Cod's "West Coast," the eastern shore of Buzzards Bay, a place unlike any other of our shorelines. Here, as though a giant bean bag had been ripped open, the very rocks of the moraine lay spilled and exposed, acre upon acre of naked granite upon the sand.

Suddenly I entered a world that was all light, planes, motion, and unfettered energy, a world of rhythmic flux. Sunlight, which had fallen in ordered vertical shafts through the woods, creating a distinct mosaic of shadows, was here broken

Rocky shoreline

Devil's Beach, East Dennis

up into a brilliant ubiquity, like constantly shattering glass. Disembodied islands and points of land hung shimmering, mirage-like, above the dark blue horizon of the bay. The sea breeze gently quartered around the compass, and whipped up little whitecaps across the water. The day had become all centrifugal, decentralized, and the weather sucked at me like a vortex.

As though to symbolize the kinetic energy of the place, a cloud of a hundred roseate terns appeared just offshore, feeding on an unseen school of silversides or young herring. Above me they were a moving swarm of motion and noise. Their sharp *chivy* calls assaulted my ears, and the horde of angled, fluttering wings flashed and glinted like knives. Beneath them the waters suddenly exploded with a school of silverside minnows chased to the surface by some unseen predator, and the terns swooped down like banshees to feed. The surface of the water burst with their rapid, wasp-like plunges down after the fish, rising and diving, rising and diving. . . .

Suddenly the morning in the calm woods seemed years away. Yet I could turn and look east to see, less than a mile off, those same solid-seeming hills I had earlier sauntered through. Only now, from the beach, they seemed covered with an ephemeral haze; now it was *they* that seemed a mirage, a false front of temporarily arrested motion.

On such a beach, solidity rapidly loses credibility. These morainal forests in all their grandeur become a mere mound of loose gravel (gravel, it is true, that sometimes runs twenty feet coarse, but gravel nonetheless) with a thin coating of cellulose. Our moraines are, after all, merely fossils of glacial movement, and their fate, under the urging of wind and wave, is eventually to move once more, to descend to the beach and become, at last, like the rocks that lay scattered all about me.

I CLIMB THE THICKLY VEGETATED RAVINE that lies between two rounded, sandy flanks on the eastern slope of Mt. Ararat, up from the National Seashore's parking lot that once served as a siding for the railroad into Provincetown. Winter is the best time for exploring the dunes—the sands are firmer, the walking easier. It has been cold and still for the past several days, and it is like walking over slightly sanded concrete, leaving no footprints. Relatively few people seek out the dunes in winter, and one can walk an entire day without seeing another soul.

Compass grass and dunes

Griffin Island, Wellfleet

Beach cottages

The owners these days tend to be from neighboring Cape towns like Dennis and Brewster, but some name signs I encounter are pure Chatham still: Nickerson and Lumpkin on my nearest neighbor's, Crowell on a beached boat.

Inside, most of these cottages are plain, even negligently spartan. Some have imported trappings of suburban rec rooms: masonite paneling, captain's chairs, coasters, "Old Philosopher" wall paintings, et cetera. But outside, all retain an enforced simplicity, a perpetually nomadic look, like dice thrown and rethrown again on the gaming table of the beach. There is little of that external, self-conscious, quaint cuteness that infects so much of the mainland's dwellings, from lobster pots on the lawns to hawser-and-pier fencing to "Cod's Little Acre" and "Our Hide-Aweigh" carved quarterboards over the garages. What there is of this is relegated mostly to the outhouses, perennial source of amusement among refugees from indoor plumbing. One has a "Lobster Potty II" sign above its door, with a genuine wooden pot mounted on the roof. The few signs attached to the cottages themselves tend to be self-deprecating—"Nauset Hilton" on a boathouse—or bristly—"Warning: Trap Gun Set" on a boarded-up window.

There is a kind of landscape humor to them as well. Their owners seem to enjoy bringing in useless artifacts of civilization and planting them around their houses: fire hydrants, newspaper boxes, "Keep Off the Grass" signs. It is a kind of inverse boasting, a reveling in their temporary freedom from the tyranny of what these objects symbolize. One owner has nailed an electric meter to the side of a wall.

Late on a late September afternoon I get out of the car and start to walk slowly, as I have done so many times this year, across the long sandy stretch of barrier beach toward the unseen sea. I come to the little wooden footbridge that spans the shallow tidal river, its two-faced current now flowing gently southward, its depth ebbing with the tide. Here, all summer, blond-haired children ran their stick races, dropping twigs or bits of marsh grass over one side of the bridge, then dashing to the other side to see the winner emerge. Their imaginations made a great tunnel of the four-foot width of that bridge—a safe tunnel with a predictable exit, and yet one whose unseen currents could, as they crossed that width of planks, sort out and change in a matter of seconds the order and fate of the passive sticks.

The children are gone now, though the alternating currents of the stream continue in their lunar rhythms, and one can only guess whether the long-abandoned sticks lie stranded somewhere bleaching on the upper limits of its course, or are unimaginably scattered and refunded into the anonymous depths of the sea itself. Such tidal streams are in a sense ambiguous frauds, having no real living head-waters, no complete natural cycle as rivers do, only an endless regurgitation and reswallowing of their own substance.

The sky is in a state of brilliant instability so characteristic of this land. At a very low altitude thin-bodied sheets of cloud race madly out to sea, while higher up, majestically aloof, a cumulus layer, like a fleet of flat-bottomed boats, floats in slow whiteness in the opposite direction. Amid all this the sun periodically breaks through and splashes in broken patterns on the sand, pursuing the cloud-shadows across the plain and the sculptured dunes of the beach. It is as though the heavens are engaged in a playful, or at least thoughtless, kind of end-of-the-season housecleaning.

The wind is clean, new, and sharp with the salt of distant spray. It scatters sand, light sticks, and dead straws of beach grass. It compels the grass clumps to draw circles around themselves in the sand, as though marking off a new domain and new episode in their endless struggle for survival, while at the same time it subtly moves the dunes which threaten always to bury whatever life they foster.

All this flurry of inanimate activity discomposes me. I feel like something left over from a bygone season, that might be swept away capriciously, deposited in the sea or buried in the sand for a dark and mindless renewal. I want things quiet and still, solemn, even gray—something to feed my inarticulate need for a sense of finality, of closure, which, it seems, can only be fed from without. There are, after all, no endings or beginnings to human things unless we make them in our imag-inations, and the imagination can only feed on facts, can only create from and transform what *is* there.

I walk on, over the bridge, across the wide central plain of the beach, on which only a trace of beach-buggy wheels are left in the moving sand. And then, about a hundred feet from the final rise of dunes, as though to startle expectation, the sea throws up an unbidden gesture. It leaps up through the narrow cleft in the dunes: a sudden surge of wave that reaches out toward me, gains for an instant the irresistible shape of a hand before its lengthening fingers sink, turn to foam and dribbles, and disappear into the sand. It is a moment's apparition, an arm spawned, shaped, thrust, amputated, and buried in the space of a few seconds. That is all. Nothing follows. But it is something, and will have to be enough. I turn and head back to the bridge, the capricious wind now at my face, now at my back, but in the end undirected and uncompelling.

Sagamore Bridge, Bourne